D0570710

Everyday Confetti

Everyday Confetti

Your Year-Round Guide *to* Celebrating Holidays and Special Occasions

KAREN EHMAN and GLYNNIS WHITWER

Revell

a division of Baker Publishing Group
Grand Rapids, Michigan

© 2014 by Karen Ehman and Glynnis Whitwer

Published by Revell
a division of Baker Publishing Group
P.O. Box 6287, Grand Rapids, MI 49516-6287
www.revellbooks.com

Printed in the United States of America

All rights reserved. No part of this publication may be reproduced, stored in a retrieval system, or transmitted in any form or by any means—for example, electronic, photocopy, recording—without the prior written permission of the publisher. The only exception is brief quotations in printed reviews.

Library of Congress Cataloging-in-Publication Data is on file at the Library of Congress, Washington, DC.

ISBN 978-0-8007-2201-2 (pbk.)

Unless otherwise indicated, Scripture quotations are from the Holy Bible, New International Version®. NIV®. Copyright © 1973, 1978, 1984, 2011 by Biblica, Inc.™ Used by permission of Zondervan. All rights reserved worldwide. www.zondervan.com

Scripture quotations labeled AMP are from the Amplified® Bible, copyright © 1954, 1958, 1962, 1964, 1965, 1987 by The Lockman Foundation. Used by permission.

Scripture quotations labeled ESV are from The Holy Bible, English Standard Version® (ESV®), copyright © 2001 by Crossway, a publishing ministry of Good News Publishers. Used by permission. All rights reserved. ESV Text Edition: 2007

Scripture quotations labeled NASB are from the New American Standard Bible®, copyright © 1960, 1962, 1963, 1968, 1971, 1972, 1973, 1975, 1977, 1995 by The Lockman Foundation. Used by permission.

Scripture quotations labeled NLT are from the Holy Bible, New Living Translation, copyright © 1996, 2004, 2007 by Tyndale House Foundation. Used by permission of Tyndale House Publishers, Inc., Carol Stream, Illinois 60188. All rights reserved.

Published in association with the literary agency of Fedd & Company, Inc., PO Box 341973, Austin, TX 78734

In keeping with biblical principles of creation stewardship, Baker Publishing Group advocates the responsible use of our natural resources. As a member of the Green Press Initiative, our company uses recycled paper when possible. The text paper of this book is composed in part of post-consumer waste.

Dedication

Karen

Patricia Wnukowski, my mother's only sister, lived in a tall brick house in Milwaukee, Wisconsin. The eight-hour car ride around the southern tip of Lake Michigan was worth it because she—and her wonderful cooking—would be waiting at the end. (Pot roast and pineapple cheesecake were my favorites!) She was interested in my life, always asking me to sing or cheerlead for her. She gently brushed the tangles out of my hair and smelled like White Shoulders perfume. Still today, she never fails to send me a handwritten card on my birthday. Aunt Patty sprinkles the confetti of kindness wherever she goes. If I ever do grow up, I want to be just like her.

Glynnis

My little Welsh grandmother, Anna Mae Owens, had braces on her legs due to polio as a girl and lived in a little one-bedroom apartment all the years I knew her. She had no money to speak of due to the fact her husband died while she was carrying my father. But in spite of all her hardships, she still found a way to make me feel loved when I visited. Whether it was tea in the afternoon, homemade macaroni and cheese, calling me her little black-eyed Susan (although my eyes are hazel), or celebrating my mud pie creations, Grandma Owens made my time with her special. My prayer is to leave a legacy like hers.

Contents

Acknowledgments

We toss a handful of confetti to celebrate and thank those who helped us take this project from a bunch of ideas—both those we have done and those swirling around in our minds—to the volume you now hold in your hands.

To our Proverbs 31 Ministries sisters under the leadership of Lysa TerKeurst: We love doing life with you and trusting God together for the ministry he has for us as a team. We are grateful for your endless encouragement and prayer support. You are all so very "graceful, godly, and ready to go." Also, a special thanks to those who shared some of your celebration ideas with the readers of this book.

To agent Esther Fedorkevich: Your professionalism and hard work along with your love of serving Jesus and enabling others to touch lives through the written word make you the best at what you do. Thanks for believing in us and in this project.

To Andrea Doering, Twila Bennett, Lindsay Davis, Lindsey Spoolstra, Cheryl Van Andel, and the rest of the fabulous team at Revell: Thank you for all of your expertise as you guided this project from idea to manuscript to a book in the store. Your tireless efforts do not go unnoticed. We love doing ministry with you!

To the many online friends we have through our own blogs and through Proverbs 31 Ministries: You are the reason we write, speak, and serve. A loud shout-out to the ones who contributed your own unique ideas to this book that helped to round it out. We appreciate the time you took to share them with all of us.

To husbands Todd E. and Tod W. and the eight Ehman and Whitwer children: Thank you for your patience as we talked on the phone brainstorming and then headed to our computers to craft our manuscript, a feat that meant a few rounds of fast food and nights of leftovers for you all. Making our homes a haven for you, celebrating your many milestones in life, or just sharing a simple meal on an ordinary day—these are among our greatest joys as wives and mothers.

And to our heavenly Father—the One who created celebrations and gave us the greatest gift of all—Jesus. We love You. May You be glorified in the pages of this book and in the lives of those who read it.

Foreword

When you hear the word "confetti," what pops into your mind? Party noise-makers and streamers, as handfuls of the glittery stuff are tossed into the air on New Year's Eve? A shower of colorful paper pieces wafting through the air as an award-winning team returns to a welcoming hometown parade? Or a scattering on your kitchen table as your family celebrates a birthday or anniversary?

The calendar is filled with special occasions and holidays that certainly call for a little confetti. But what about ordinary days? Those seemingly routine days when the calendar doesn't indicate an occasion to buy a card, bake a cake, or toss some confetti? By bringing a little confetti to an otherwise ordinary day, we can make it a celebration. A celebration of life, of each other, and, most importantly, of God's goodness.

Our desire with this book is to spark your creativity and provide you with ideas for planning and implementing wonderful holiday and holy day celebrations with your loved ones. But we don't want to stop there. We hope that with a little ingenuity and a slight shift in your spiritual perspective, you will learn to toss a little confetti into the everyday too—to be on the lookout for days and ways to make the ordinary *extraordinary*.

As the caregivers of our homes and families, something deep within us calls us to pause and savor the moment we are in. Maybe it's because there were too many years that are a blur now. Too many moments we wished would hurry up and pass. Those are the times of regret.

As we look into the faces of children growing up too quickly, of parents growing older, of friends packing to move, we often want time to stop while we breathe in the holiness of the moment God has given.

Remember this moment, our heart whispers. *Remember what this feels like.*

We hold on to a tiny frame just a minute longer, rest our head on his chest and sigh, grab a wrinkled hand and draw it to our cheek, and gaze into eyes we adore.

Life goes by too quickly, and at the end of the year we can look back and wish the simple moments had been celebrated more. We wish there'd been a few more pauses. We wish we'd made more opportunities to look at someone we love and say, with words and actions, "You matter. I value you."

Not the big flashy moments. Not the expensive trips. But the humble, family times that declare what's really important. What makes us *us*. The everyday moments are the ones that are treasured in the hearts of those we love.

It's the little touches that say, "I remembered." It's celebrating effort. Rejoicing together in success. Supporting each other when discouraged. These are the times that weave our hearts together.

Often those times turn into traditions. And there's an amazing benefit of traditions—they establish family unity. They declare, "This is who we are . . . what we believe in . . . what we stand for." Traditions give us a sense of belonging.

Some women excel at these spontaneous family moments. They can whip together a celebration with a box cake mix, some gummy worms, and a paper bag. Then there are the rest of us, who do better with some planning. Don't be discouraged if that's you. We understand. That's why we wrote this book.

Our home can be a place of nurturing, a place where children grow up confident in their worth, a place where a husband feels respected and a friend feels loved, a place where God is honored.

In a world where our schedules leave us frazzled and comparisons leave us wanting, where children come home belittled and husbands can feel "less than," don't we all need a place to feel safe? To feel accepted? To feel honored?

As you read through this book, we hope you'll be inspired to celebrate more everyday moments. To pause in the midst of a busy holiday and remember what's really important. And to love your family with more intentionality.

Life is filled with moments to treasure and to celebrate. Together, let's sprinkle confetti on these treasured moments, making sure to leave a layer on those we celebrate with and for, and on those God calls us to love on in His name.

Thank you for joining us on this journey.

In Jesus's love,
Karen and Glynnis

PART 1

Everyday Celebrations

Rejoice always, pray continually, give thanks in all circumstances; for this is God's will for you in Christ Jesus.

1 Thessalonians 5:16–18

*C*elebrations are markers in our lives. Birthdays, engagements, baptisms, graduations, a promotion, a part in the Christmas pageant, or the first lost tooth—every milestone, event, and accomplishment should be celebrated and remembered.

But what about the other days? The in-between days? What about an ordinary Wednesday?

Time goes by so quickly. But with a little imagination, creativity, and a sprinkling of confetti, we can make the most of life's little moments and create memories in our hearts that will last a lifetime.

In this chapter we want to share small things that have made a difference in our families. But we're also sharing creative ideas from other people. No one can pull off all these ideas, so pick the ones that seem to be a good fit for *you*. We've also included recipe ideas to help you celebrate. We've intentionally made the recipes simple so you can spend less time preparing and more time with those you love.

Celebrating the Everyday Joys

FAMILY DINNER TIME

Steaming bowls of comfort waiting to be passed. The day's humorous stories ready to be shared. Hands held. Heads bowed. The family supper table. What was once a familiar routine in families now threatens to become a lost art.

We know busy schedules make it hard for family meals to happen consistently. Here are some practical tips for establishing a habit and making it a beneficial experience:

Schedule your dinners in advance. Consider each one an appointment with the most important people in your life.

Create a menu. A little forethought can eliminate stress and overspending and can assure a healthier selection of food.

Get the family involved. Ask your family what they'd like to eat. If they are invested in the menu, they are more likely to help with a good attitude. Plus, if it's something they love, they'll want to come (this is especially important with teenagers).

No screens. Period. Make sure anything with an "on" button is in the "off" position, or at least is not at the table.

Plan the discussion. This might sound contrived, but it's better to have a backup plan than to have silence or complaining. One simple way to start conversation is to have everyone share their high point and low point of the day. Or ask them to tell about one new fact they learned in school or something they saw on the internet they had questions about. Perhaps place some discussion prompts on slips of paper and draw one each night to get the conversation going. Let every member of the family come up with some suggestions. Adults might ask questions about what dreams everyone has for the future. Kids might inquire about what their parents' lives were like growing up. Even random and somewhat silly questions are totally fine, such as, "If you were a color what color would you be and why?" or "If you could meet any cartoon character who would it be and why?" or "What snack food would you most hate to have to give up for life—and if you were paid money to do so, how much would it take for you to give it up?"

> Be merry, really merry.
> The life of a true Christian should be a perpetual jubilee, a prelude to the festivals of eternity.
>
> ~ *Theophane Venard*

CREATE A FAMILY HONOR PLATE

The dinner table is a perfect place to celebrate a milestone or special occasion. It can also serve as a way to praise a child for a job well done or to honor a family member for displaying a Christlike character quality. Some families even use a special plate to add to the festivities of such honoring times.

If you would like to begin this tradition in your own home, purchase a dinner plate in a bright color that will only be used by a family member on the night of an accomplishment. Or purchase a retro or antique plate if your family would enjoy such a piece. You could even create one at a local ceramics shop just for your clan to use.

So—how to use it? Did a child make the tennis team? Land a great grade on a difficult paper or project? They get to eat their meal on the special family plate.

But don't just use the plate for academic, athletic, or extracurricular achievements. Go beyond. Also honor family members—both kids and parents—for displaying acts of kindness or character. Did they rake the neighbors' yard without being asked? Give up their place in line to a frenzied mom with a crying baby? Did they display perseverance by studying diligently for a big exam even though the grade was not as high as they'd hoped? Honor them with dinner on the family plate.

You may also want to check out our friend Michelle Weber's website. She has created a unique way to encourage and honor family members at dinner for godly character qualities. The Family Enrichment Tool Kit incorporates the fruit of the Spirit, the very virtues of Christ.

The tool kit includes a simple but effective program presented on an audio CD, a Family Honor Plate (personalized with your family's name), a Table Thyme set that includes 250 discussion starters and questions, and a free membership to a curriculum-based character education site so parents can pull up character-specific historical stories of those who have shown great character to prepare for enlightening conversation at dinner. Imagine having specific information to share about Albert Einstein or Abraham Lincoln the evening one of your children (hey, Mom and Dad can earn it too) receives the honor plate for showing perseverance.

To summarize the program, parents are taught to:

Catch their children doing good things and making smart choices based on their character; they'll find these things because now they are looking for them.

Celebrate those good choices and behaviors (based on character and actions, not "successes") by presenting their child's meal on the Family Honor Plate. Let the child be the "star" as they listen to why they are being honored and the effect it had on others. The audience is their family and the stage is the dinner table. Siblings learn and are inspired as they see their brother or sister being celebrated for their good choices or behavior.

Connect with their family as they bring everyone together at the dinner table not just to eat but to learn the joy of gathering, building each other up, sharing, and growing as a family. Pick a Table Thyme card and enjoy an evening where each person has the opportunity to share their opinions, thoughts, and desires. Learn how to create engaging dialogue among family members. Parents will begin to see inside their children's hearts, and their children will see inside their parents'. When people get to know each other better they feel more connected and relationships grow stronger. The result? The family genuinely enjoys coming together at the dinner table, and family mealtime becomes a priority to everyone. The benefits are endless.

If you would like more information, you may obtain it at www.Family EnrichmentToolkit.com.

Establish a Weekly Family Night (or Morning or Afternoon)

As moms of busy children, we know how hard it is to carve out time with family. But in most homes, it is possible to set aside time every week to strengthen your family unity, to turn your hearts toward God, and to have fun in the process. The key is commitment, consistency, and a small amount of creativity.

Don't worry about it being exactly right, and don't compare your family's plans with anyone else's. There's no perfect day, perfect amount of time, or perfect agenda. Maybe your family only has Saturday mornings, or after church on Sundays, or Tuesday nights. Grab that time and try to make it nonnegotiable.

We think it's always easier to start simply when trying to establish a habit. So don't set expectations you can't continue to meet. A little food, a little conversation, some laughter, and you've got a memory in the making.

A few years ago, I (Glynnis) met a pastor's wife at a small church in Louisiana. This grandma of many was discussing her dinner menu for later that day. The guest list numbered around twenty and included children, grandchildren, and a few friends invited into the fold. Was it someone's birthday? Or anniversary? I was curious.

"No," she answered. "It's just Sunday dinner. We do this every week. It's how we keep our family connected."

What a wonderful practice. A simple dinner. A standing invitation. A reason to reconnect with friends and family after a busy week.

What might this look like in your home? The type of food doesn't matter as much as making enough to feed a few extra friends who might be invited.

Maybe your special family time is you and your husband . . . or maybe it's a passel of children and grandkids. No matter the size of the gathering, the fanciness of your table, or the spot on the calendar, establishing time together with people you love is worth the investment.

Here are some ideas you can try as you gather your people:

Devotional time. Pick a short passage of the Bible to read together. Depending on the ages of your children, take turns coming up with a few discussion questions. Keep this simple to help make the Bible accessible to every member of your family. Close with a short prayer thanking God for His Word and message to you tonight. Pray also for others.

Make-your-own _____ night. Get the family involved in making dinner. One idea is make-your-own pizza. Using French bread or hoagie rolls as your base, set out an assortment of toppings, pizza sauce, and cheese and let everyone assemble their own creation. You might also try a salad bar, sub sandwiches, or Cincinnati chili (with optional five toppings).

Board games. Board games can be expensive, but compare their cost with taking your family out to the movies and you might have a new perspective. Some of our favorites include Ticket to Ride, Apples to Apples, and Imaginiff.

Arts and crafts. A craft project stimulates creativity and camaraderie. Paint flower pots, color eggs at Easter, decorate cookies at Christmas, or make pinecone bird feeders using peanut butter.

Read out loud. Pick a book to read through as a family. This is a family tradition your children will appreciate (coming from a woman—Glynnis—whose mother read faithfully to her). Some family-friendly selections include *The Trumpet of the Swan, The Secret Garden, Mrs. Piggle-Wiggle,* and any of the Chronicles of Narnia series.

Family sleepover. When our (Glynnis) children were small, we'd spread blankets, sleeping bags, and pillows on the floor of the master bedroom for a sleepover. There was something special about ending the night together . . . sort of like a camping experience without the dirt.

· · · · · · · · · **Lysa TerKeurst** · · · · · · · · ·

Proverbs 31 Ministries

Have you ever felt guilty for not having sit-down family devotions? I have. It's not that I haven't tried, but somewhere between the less-than-enthusiastic response I would sometimes get and my own inconsistency, the guilt comes. If you've ever struggled with this, like I do, I might have a solution—everyday conversations about God.

I've done a lot wrong as a mom, but one thing I've done right is to celebrate God in everyday life. By weaving God and His truth throughout the fabric of the simple things every day, it makes Him more real, applicable, and touchable. Here are three ways I do this:

When something goes right—we stop and praise God for His provision.

When something goes wrong—we look for how this might be evidence of God's protection.

When we need wisdom for how to handle situations, we look for it in God's Word and discuss ways to apply it.

If we talk about God in our everyday lives, it creates a sense of celebration of His presence. And that's the best kind of family devotion there is!

SIBLINGS' NIGHT

Karen

For the first decade of parenting, we lived in a very tiny home. All three of our kids, ages two through nine, shared the same bedroom. A triple bunk bed and one shared dresser meant big sister had little brothers' Hot Wheels and Batman PJs right alongside her sparkly lip gloss and jewelry box. When we were finally able to move into a bigger home with two bedrooms for the kids, we thought they'd be thrilled. But while they loved the look of their individual rooms, when nighttime came they wanted to be together. In fact, for the first month or so the boys dragged their pillows and blankets into their sister's room and slept on her floor!

We noticed that the kids had a little routine to their nighttime activities. They'd get drinks of water, Kenna would read the boys a story, and then she would sing them a song from our church camp called "Goodnight Boys, Sleep Tight Boys." That tradition was something they didn't want to give up!

Our living situation eventually morphed into everyone in their own rooms. However, a few nights every month, until our daughter moved out at age eighteen, they would hold Siblings' Night. They'd fix a snack and retreat to Kenna's bedroom to watch a movie with NO PARENTS ALLOWED. Then the boys would sleep on her floor and she would lull them into dreamland by singing her goodnight song.

Even now, when she returns for a holiday from her home five states away, you will find the tradition of Siblings' Night taking place in our guestroom—with her on the twin bed and the big, strapping, teenage boys on her floor!

RECIPES FOR FAMILY GATHERINGS

Need something easy to feed a crowd? These two recipes can be prepared ahead. Add a fresh green salad and hot French bread, and you have a family feast.

Creamy Italian Chicken over Rice

8	boneless, skinless chicken breast halves
1 pkg.	dry Italian salad dressing mix
¼ c.	water
8 oz.	cream cheese
1 (10¾ oz.) can	cream of chicken soup
1 (4 oz.) can	mushrooms, drained

Lightly grease slow cooker and place chicken breasts inside. Combine Italian dressing and water and pour over chicken. Cover slow cooker and cook on low for 4–5 hours. Then combine cream cheese and condensed soup in a saucepan and heat on medium until melted. Whisk together to remove lumps (there may still be some). Stir in mushrooms and pour over chicken. Cover and cook another 30 minutes or so. Serve over rice. Serves 6–8.

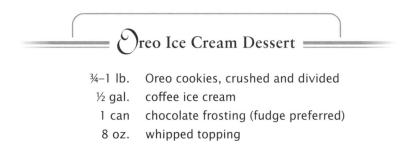

Oreo Ice Cream Dessert

¾–1 lb. Oreo cookies, crushed and divided
½ gal. coffee ice cream
1 can chocolate frosting (fudge preferred)
8 oz. whipped topping

Spread half of crushed Oreos on the bottom of a 9 x 13 pan. Slice ice cream and cover Oreos evenly. Warm frosting in microwave by removing the foil cover and heating the container for 15 seconds on high. Stir. Continue heating in 15-second intervals until pourable. Pour frosting over ice cream. Spread whipped topping over frosting, and top with remaining crushed Oreos. Freeze at least 2 hours before serving. Serves 10–12.

NAME DAY

In Bible days, names had great significance. Parents named their children with great intentionality, but not always for the same reasons. Sara and Abraham named their son Isaac, which means "laughter," because they laughed when God said they'd have a child. Isaac named his son Jacob, from a root word that means "to follow," because he was the second-born twin, but the name also had connotations of a conniver, because during birth he grasped his brother's heel.

God also renamed people when their purpose or identity changed. Jacob is an example of that when God changed his name to Israel (Gen. 32:28) after he wrestled with a man who represented God. Jesus renamed one of his disciples from Simon (meaning "he has heard") to Peter (meaning "stone" or "rock").

Because names have traditionally held such significance, there's an old European tradition that assigns a name to each day of the year, making it "Name Day." So not only are you celebrated on your birthday, but there's another day to celebrate with every other Karen (April 29 in Italy) or Glynnis (October 14 in the United States). To find your Name Day, there is a fun website that offers an American calendar: americanname daycalendar.com.

Whether or not you were named with as much intentionality as Isaac, Jacob, or Jesus (meaning "He who saves"), you can still celebrate your name on Name Day. Here are some suggestions on how to do so:

Name acronym. On each family member's Name Day, write their name vertically on the left side of a sheet of paper and leave it out in the open. Then have the rest of the family write descriptive words starting with each letter. Here's what Glynnis wrote about Karen, for example:

K–Kind

A–Astute

R–Reliable

E–Effervescent

N–Nice

Make a name necklace or bracelet. Go to a craft store and pick out letter beads, plus extra beads or charms, to make a necklace or bracelet for the Name Day celebrant. This would've been the only way Glynnis would've had anything personalized growing up.

Photo collage using initials. On Glynnis's son Robbie's birthday, a friend surprised him with a photo collage using his Facebook photos. She found the letter R made from stretched canvas, glued on the photos so they overlapped, and painted clear varnish on top to protect them. This idea can be expanded to include the entire name and feature photos of interests as well as people.

Celebrate your loved one's name heritage. Where did their name originate? On their Name Day, prepare a special treat from the country from which their name originated. For example, Glynnis is Welsh and means "from the valley." Karen could make her Welsh tea cakes. To search for a name's heritage, invest in a baby name book or visit the internet and search for a specific name.

2

Celebrating Birthdays

Birthdays and other occasions are about so much more than cake and ice cream. The way you make the birthday boy or girl feel is what's important. A few simple personal touches will make them feel extra special.

BIRTHDAY TABLECLOTH TRADITIONS

Invest in a plastic tablecloth you can use year after year. With permanent markers, have the guests write their names in a circle starting in the center. Each year bring out the tablecloth for guests to sign and enjoy how the signatures change over the years.

Or purchase a clear plastic tablecloth. When it is time for a birthday, scatter pictures of the birthday boy or girl from years past on the table, along with some confetti. Place the clear tablecloth on top, and you have an instant decorated tabletop! You can also use this same idea for anniversaries or showers.

BIRTHDAY WEEK

We celebrate the entire week of each person's birth (instead of just the day). Because our family has four kids, being the absolute center of attention for an entire week is a BIG hit. We don't do something over-the-top every day—it's all in the presentation. I'll buy special treats that the birthday child likes, they get to pick out the weekend movie, and select a few fun activities (like going to the park or the zoo). Each day I try to draw attention to them as the birthday boy/girl, and will say, "Because it's the week of (fill in the blank), we're getting doughnuts," or "Since it's the week of (fill in the blank), we're going on a walk to get the mail," or whatever tiny treat I have planned for the day. When I phrase it this way, even the tiniest of activities becomes a celebration! Then on the morning of their birthday, they wake up to streamers, balloons, homemade signs/cards, and their "(fill in the blank) is the BEST because . . ." list, which the entire family creates. It's always such a fun way to celebrate the gift they are to our family!

Stephanie H.

THIRD BIRTHDAY

Glynnis

This is the age when children start anticipating their birthdays. My son Dylan started planning his third birthday party soon after his second. He was consumed with his guest list and, of course, his gift list. I'll never forget the day my father corrected two-year-old Dylan for some minor infraction, and Dylan replied with a pout: "You aren't coming to my birthday party!" (The worst punishment imaginable!) To which my father replied, "Please, I really want to come." Dylan thought for a minute and said, "OK, call me every day to see if I've changed my mind!" Of course, Dylan did change his mind.

Consider having a small party for your three-year-old with the theme of three. For example, have guests bring tricycles and tie three helium balloons to each. Serve three cookies, three chicken nuggets, three carrot strips, and so on.

HALF BIRTHDAY

When our daughter was growing up, we celebrated her half birthday in a specific way. On her half birthday she was given a new responsibility, with the explanation that as we grow older there will be more responsibility given to each of us.

When she was a freshman theater major in college, this tradition helped her. As part of the tech crew, she and the rest of the team were responsible for mopping the floor at the end of the night. None of the other techs knew how to do this. That night she ended up teaching them how to properly mop a floor.

Half birthdays throughout the years helped our girl learn how to wash clothes, wash dishes, clean bathrooms, vacuum, dust, and basically how to clean and take care of a home.

Our daughter knew that each year she would get a new responsibility on her half birthday, but when her birthday came around, there would also be a new privilege.

Dawn W.

· · · · · · · · · **Nicki Koziarz** · · · · · · ·

Proverbs 31 Ministries

Birthdays are a big deal to kids. As a mom, I knew once my kids got old enough to remember things, I wanted to create a special birthday tradition.

But, I can be a last-minute-idea type of girl. So the night before my oldest daughter turned four, I frantically began to try to think of something I could do to create a special birthday memory for her.

We had nothing creative in our house! All I could find were paper plates and a Sharpie. And so began the Birthday Plates.

That night I took a dozen or so paper plates and a Sharpie and got to work. On each of the plates, I wrote things like: "Happy Birthday!" "It's your special day!" "We love you!" "You are awesome!" I decorated the plates with hearts and smiley faces. Then I placed the plates on a trail from her bedroom door all the way to the breakfast table.

In the morning when she woke up she was so excited about the messages on each of the plates and followed the trail to the table. On the final plate I placed her breakfast, and she LOVED it!

Now we have three girls and the excitement of the tradition continues. Every year on the night before their birthdays they each say, "Mommy, don't forget my birthday plates!"

GOLDEN BIRTHDAY

For another birthday tradition, celebrate a "golden birthday." This simply is the year that the day of the month your birthday falls on matches your age. So, someone born on the eleventh would have his or her golden birthday the year they turn eleven. Of course, after thirty-one there are no more golden birthdays because you are out of days of the month! For fun, give the birthday boy or girl items in quantities the same as their golden birthday. Maybe seventeen mini candy bars or twenty-three peanut M&Ms.

> **Life becomes precious and more special to us when we look for the little everyday miracles and get excited about the privileges of simply being human.**
>
> ~ *Tim Hansel*

DOUBLE-DIGIT BIRTHDAY DECATHLON

When your son or daughter turns ten, hold a double-digit decathlon! Plan ten crazy games to be played Olympic style as a silly decathlon. These might include pin the nose on the birthday boy or girl (have a headshot of them blown up at a print shop and cut noses out of construction paper), a backwards foot race, a race rolling Ping-Pong balls with a spoon, a shot put competition with water balloons, or a javelin throw with empty wrapping paper tubes. Anything goes! Serve stadium-style food such as hot dogs, nachos, and popcorn. Be sure to award gold medals to everyone—bags full of chocolate gold coins.

LET THEM EAT CAKE

While most food on birthdays tends to be of the guest of honor's choosing (after all, it is their big day), sometimes we can get in a rut with what kind of cake to make. Here are some of our favorites that win rave reviews every time:

Chocolate Surprise Cake

The surprise is the secret ingredient—mayonnaise! Don't let it fool you. This cake is FABULOUS!

• *Cake*

2 oz.	bittersweet chocolate, chopped
⅔ c.	unsweetened cocoa powder
1¾ c.	boiling water
2¾ c.	all-purpose flour
1¼ tsp.	baking soda
¼ tsp.	baking powder
1 c.	sugar
1 c.	dark brown sugar, packed
1⅓ c.	real mayonnaise
2 lg.	eggs
1 tsp.	vanilla extract

• *Frosting*

10 oz.	bittersweet chocolate, chopped
1½ c.	unsalted butter, room temperature
3 c.	powdered sugar
1 Tbs.	vanilla extract

Preheat oven to 350°F. Butter and flour two 9-inch or three 8-inch round pans or spray with cooking spray meant for baking, such as Baker's Secret, not just an oil spray.

For cake: combine chopped chocolate and cocoa powder in a medium bowl. Add boiling water and blend until melted and smooth.

Combine flour, baking soda, and baking powder in another bowl. Set aside. Using an electric mixer, beat both sugars along with the mayonnaise in a large bowl until blended. Add eggs one at a time. Add melted chocolate. Stir in vanilla. Add flour mixture slowly, beating well and occasionally scraping down sides of bowl. Divide batter equally among prepared cake pans.

Bake cakes until tester inserted into center comes out clean, 30–32 minutes for 8-inch pans and slightly longer for 9-inch pans. Cool pans on wire racks. Run a knife around cake edges to loosen. Flip onto cooling racks.

For frosting: melt chopped chocolate in a double boiler (or in a metal bowl that will fit nicely in a saucepan; place bowl over saucepan of simmering water), stirring until chocolate is smooth. Carefully remove from heat and let melted chocolate cool slightly as you stir it occasionally.

Beat softened butter in a large bowl. Gradually add in powdered sugar and beat until well blended. Beat in vanilla. Add melted chocolate and beat until smooth, occasionally scraping down sides of bowl. Frost the cooled cake and enjoy!

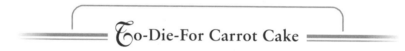

To-Die-For Carrot Cake

In a large bowl, mix together:

2 c.	sugar
1½ c.	oil
4	eggs

Blend until smooth. Add in the following:

2 c.	all-purpose flour
1 tsp.	salt
2 tsp.	baking soda
2 tsp.	cinnamon
½ tsp.	nutmeg
¼ tsp.	cloves
3 c.	carrots, shredded
¾ c.	raisins
½ c.	walnuts, chopped

Pour into two greased and floured 9-inch round cake pans. Bake at 350°F for 35–40 minutes or until a tester comes out clean. Do not over bake. Cool slightly and then loosen the edges with a butter knife. Turn out onto rack to cool while you make the frosting.

• *Frosting*

8 oz.	cream cheese, softened
½ c.	butter (no substitutions)
2⅔ c.	powdered sugar (or more)
1 tsp.	vanilla

Beat all ingredients until smooth, adding more powdered sugar if needed. Frost cooled cake and serve.

THIRTEENTH BIRTHDAY

Becoming a teenager is a rite of passage for all children. Acknowledge this day with a special event.

Glynnis

When our boys turned thirteen, my husband took each one of them on a surprise trip that he planned for the two of them. One went on a business trip out of state with some extra days tacked on, another hiked the Grand Canyon, and the third went away for a guys' weekend.

A friend told of her son's thirteenth birthday when her husband planned a special men's-only luncheon, and invited men who were important in her son's life. The guest list included the pastor of their church, a grandfather, an uncle, and a few other male adult friends who had seen her son grow up. Each one told what they respected about the young teen, and gave some words of encouragement.

Thirteen is a special year for a girl as well. Consider this idea:

Our oldest daughter will be turning thirteen in a few months, and we have a ring with three hearts on it picked out. We're going to take her to dinner and explain her heart is in the middle of our hearts and we want to hold her heart until God sends her husband to hold it for us. She will wear it on her ring finger until she marries.

Karen R.

OLDER BIRTHDAYS

For our daughter's sixteenth birthday, I emailed people who had loved her and known her throughout her life. This included teachers, family friends, her friends, grandparents, extended family, and so forth. I asked them to email or mail me a letter addressed to her with a favorite Bible verse, a funny or sentimental story about her, their wishes for her as she continued to grow in the Lord, and anything else they could think of that they would like to say.

I put these together in a scrapbook and surprised her with it on her birthday. She was to read one a day for the month of her birthday. It was such a blessing to her, and she was surprised by the number of people who reached out to her in love.

Gretchen S.

On my son's twenty-first birthday, I contacted twenty-one people to call/text/email him at various times throughout the day. He found it to be a fun annoyance!

Linda N.

HOLIDAY BIRTHDAYS

My daughter was born on December 23. With a birthday so close to Christmas, making the day special is sometimes challenging. We started a tradition of a birthday tree for her. By the first of December each year, we decorate an all-white, tabletop-size tree in bright colors with a huge pink polka dot bow—the birthday tree! Any birthday presents are placed under this tree. It helps to distinguish her birthday from the overshadowing Christmas season.

She is now a junior at college. This past year, she was turning twenty-one, and asked if I would bring the tree to her at Thanksgiving. She wanted to have her birthday tree at school because she had missed it in previous years. She LOVES the Christmas season, and has stated she cannot imagine having a birthday at any other time of the year!

Becky A.

Seemingly small expressions of kindness can soften hearts and bear eternal fruit. As we love others with actions and in truth, God is faithful to bring forth a harvest. When we extend His love and kindness to others, they can see His perfect love, salvation, and provision. Our rewards blossom in our soul as God fills us with His joy and peace.

Let your light shine before others, that they may see your good deeds and glorify your Father in heaven.

Matthew 5:16

• • • • • • • • • • Sharon Sloan • • • • • • • • •
Proverbs 31 Ministries

Birthday Outreach

And let us consider how we may spur one another on toward love and good deeds.

Hebrews 10:24

When our children were very young, we were inspired by another Christian family in our community who put love into action. Following their lead, for our birthdays that year, rather than asking for birthday gifts for ourselves, we requested new library books for a Christian school in New Orleans that had been devastated by Hurricane Katrina. Our family and friends responded with enthusiasm and great generosity. In total, our little family received almost two hundred new books for the school after we had celebrated all four of our birthdays.

The following year our birthday ministry outreach was by theme. Our son, Joshua, chose basketball and our daughter, Gabrielle, chose flip-flops. Their party guests brought new basketballs and gift cards for footwear that we then donated to Rock Ministries of Philadelphia, which ministers to at-risk young men and young women of Philadelphia's inner city. Gabrielle's guests generously gave more than four hundred dollars in footwear gift cards, and Joshua's guests donated thirty new basketballs for the young men at Rock Ministries.

The next year Joshua invited his friends to take a tour of Lincoln Financial Field in Philadelphia (home of the Philadelphia Eagles) for his birthday. He extended the invitation to some of the youth from Rock Ministries and they joined us for a fun day of football. It really made the day special for all of us to have those honored guests with us.

• • • • • • • • • • We Are Family • • • • • • • • • •

We've learned that God creates families in unique and special ways. For example, God chose to give my husband and me (Glynnis) three children the "traditional" way. But then He decided that wasn't enough. And He added the next two children via a plane flight from Liberia, Africa, to Phoenix, Arizona. I'm convinced God doesn't see the same boundaries we do. He just sees children who need a family and families who need children.

In this section, we have a few ideas to share if God has crafted your family in an unconventional way.

Every year we celebrate the date each child's adoption was finalized. We ask them what they want to do as a fun activity and take them out to dinner. It's a special time with just my husband, me, and that child. On the day we went to court to finalize their adoption, we invited family and friends to go to court with us and then out to eat to celebrate afterwards.

Kim T.

We celebrate Family Anniversary Day. That is the day our family became complete, with the addition of three very young siblings by adoption. We already had three much older sons, and thought we were getting ready to have an empty nest, until we said yes to an emergency foster care placement. We've celebrated Family Anniversary Day differently every year—for example, a trip to the zoo, horseback riding, or taking a train trip. This year, our ninth Family Anniversary, we are planning an event where everyone will produce an oil painting. (We have lots of talented artists in our expanded family, now including daughters-in-law and grandsons.)

Mardie B.

We have two daughters that we adopted from two different families in the foster care system in our county. They were both older children, so they knew all the details of the adoption. We celebrate several dates to commemorate them becoming members of our family. First, we celebrate the "Gotcha Day," which is the day they were placed into our care. Then we celebrate the "Adoption Day" which is the date of the actual adoption. We do something significant for that specific child.

Ann G.

3

Spiritual Milestones

While birthdays and anniversaries are important, there's another category of milestones to recognize and celebrate, and those are spiritual. A child's first communion, a declaration of faith, a baptism, or an adult's recommitment to the faith of his or her childhood . . . these events are life-changing. As we highlight the significance of these events in our loved ones' lives, we are rejoicing with heaven.

We also want to remember how God has answered our prayers. The Old Testament records how God grieved when His people forgot His faithfulness. And His people suffered spiritually when they forgot the greatness of their God. Let's establish habits of gratefulness for what God has done in our lives and in the lives of our loved ones.

> Let this be a sign among you, so that when your children ask later, saying, "What do these stones mean to you?"
>
> Joshua 4:6 NASB

BOOK OF REMEMBRANCE

It's never too late to record God's faithfulness. Our friend Lisa T. told us about her family's practice to record prayer requests in a book. Then God's answer is recorded for later generations to come and "see what the Lord has done for us!" For an affordable way to start this practice, simply purchase a beautiful journal and keep it out in the open. You might make this part of your family dinner practice as well.

STONES OF JORDAN MEMORIAL

We created our own "Stones of Jordan" memorial (read Joshua 4) with a large silver platter we use as a centerpiece at our dining table or side table. I got some river stones at a local landscape business. Each of our family selected one stone and told of something they were thankful for as remembrance of God's goodness in our lives. Then we used a permanent marker to write a couple of words on each rock to capture the event it represents.

Tanya J.

SPIRITUAL BIRTHDAY CELEBRATION

Although birthday parties are usually given by family and friends of the birthday boy or girl, this one is hosted instead by the one celebrating! Think about your spiritual birthday, the day you decided to give your life to Christ. If you don't remember the exact day, just pick a day in that season and let the planning begin!

Host a dinner, inviting people who have been important in your spiritual life. Perhaps it's a small group leader, Sunday school teacher, Bible study leader, or a friend who first told you about Jesus. Also invite others who have been encouraging to you spiritually along your life's journey.

After dinner, have yourself an old-fashioned prayer meeting! Have everyone bring a favorite Bible verse to read and share why it is so special to them. The "birthday" boy or girl tells each guest what they have meant to his or her spiritual growth. End with a time of sharing prayer requests and prayer, and then enjoy the apple cake below. What a unique and blessed birthday party!

Bible Apple Cake

For fun, hand out this recipe to your guests written on a recipe card, with Proverbs 7:2 along the top: "Keep my commands and you will live; guard my teachings as the apple of your eye."

1 c.	Judges 5:25 (butter)
2 c.	Jeremiah 6:20 (sugar)
6	Isaiah 10:14 (eggs)

3½ c.	1 Kings 4:22 (flour)
½ tsp.	Leviticus 2:13 (salt)
2 tsp.	1 Corinthians 5:6 (baking powder)
¼ tsp.	each of 1 Kings 10:2 (3 spices)
1 c.	Genesis 24:20 (water)
1 Tbs.	Exodus 16:31 (honey)
½ c.	1 Samuel 25:18 (raisins or chopped figs)
1½ c.	Proverbs 7:2 (apple, chopped and peeled)
1 c.	Genesis 43:11 (nuts, chopped)

Cream softened butter and sugar. Add eggs, one at a time. Sift together flour, salt, baking powder, and spices (cinnamon, nutmeg, and allspice). Mix honey with water and add to butter mixture, alternating with dry ingredients. Stir in raisins or figs, apple, and nuts. Pour into greased loaf pan. Bake at 375°F for 50–60 minutes or until a tester inserted in the center comes out clean.

CELEBRATING THROUGH GIVING

For my son's spiritual birthday, he gets a dollar for every year he has been a Christian. He has to use the money for God's Kingdom and not himself.

Jacci S.

PRAYER SHAWLS

I love to give friends and family prayer shawls! I crochet them myself and pray over the person or family as I go. I have given them to friends before surgeries, and to my grown kids. My daughters have told me that they love to wrap up in the shawl and feel my love. It reminds them that I pray for them often!

Beth T.

RECIPE FOR SPIRITUAL MILESTONES

Inviting family and friends to your home to celebrate spiritual milestones multiplies your joy. As you host a gathering after a ceremony, consider continuing the spiritual theme with what you serve. Here are some ideas to honor the Source and Reason for the celebration. Consider hosting a meal featuring foods commonly eaten in biblical times, and posting these Scripture verses on your serving table.

BEVERAGE

Living Water. "Jesus answered her, 'If you knew the gift of God and who it is that asks you for a drink, you would have asked him and he would have given you living water'" (John 4:10).

BREAD

Bread of Life. "Then Jesus declared, 'I am the bread of life. Whoever comes to me will never go hungry, and whoever believes in me will never be thirsty'" (John 6:35).

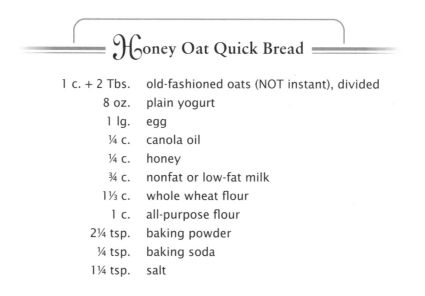

Honey Oat Quick Bread

1 c. + 2 Tbs.	old-fashioned oats (NOT instant), divided
8 oz.	plain yogurt
1 lg.	egg
¼ c.	canola oil
¼ c.	honey
¾ c.	nonfat or low-fat milk
1⅓ c.	whole wheat flour
1 c.	all-purpose flour
2¼ tsp.	baking powder
¼ tsp.	baking soda
1¼ tsp.	salt

Preheat oven to 375°F. Grease a 9 x 5-inch loaf pan and sprinkle 1 tablespoon oats across the bottom. Blend together 1 cup oats, yogurt, egg, oil, honey, and milk. In a separate bowl, stir together flours, baking powder, baking soda, and salt. Combine flour and oatmeal mixture, blending gently but thoroughly. Pour into greased pan. Sprinkle remaining tablespoon of oats across the top. Bake for 40–50 minutes or until lightly browned and sounds hollow when tapped.

ENTREE

Word of God. "Jesus answered, 'It is written: "Man shall not live on bread alone, but on every word that comes from the mouth of God"'" (Matt. 4:4). "'My food,' said Jesus, 'is to do the will of him who sent me and to finish his work'" (John 4:34).

Chicken Stew

with Walnuts, Raisins, and Pomegranate Glaze

2 Tbs.	butter, divided
2 Tbs.	olive oil, divided
2 lbs.	boneless skinless chicken breasts, cut into 1-inch pieces
1 c.	onion, chopped
5 Tbs.	pomegranate molasses
2 c.	chicken stock
1 c.	walnut pieces, chopped small
1 c.	raisins
2 Tbs.	sugar
½ tsp.	turmeric
¼ tsp.	cinnamon
¼ tsp.	ground nutmeg
¼ tsp.	ground black pepper
	salt

Brown chicken in 1 tablespoon of butter and 1 tablespoon of olive oil. Remove from pan. Add remaining butter and oil to the pan and sauté onions. Put chicken back into the pan and add remaining ingredients, blending well. Cook uncovered over medium heat for 15 minutes to thicken the sauce, then cover, reduce heat, and simmer another 30–40 minutes, or until chicken is tender. Serve with brown rice, couscous, or grain of your choice. Serves 6.

> **You make known to me the path of life; you will fill me with joy in your presence, with eternal pleasures at your right hand.**
>
> ~ *Psalm 16:11*

Dessert

The Lord Is Good. "Taste and see that the LORD is good; blessed is the one who takes refuge in him" (Ps. 34:8).

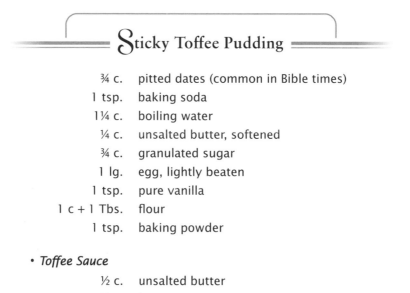

Sticky Toffee Pudding

¾ c.	pitted dates (common in Bible times)
1 tsp.	baking soda
1¼ c.	boiling water
¼ c.	unsalted butter, softened
¾ c.	granulated sugar
1 lg.	egg, lightly beaten
1 tsp.	pure vanilla
1 c + 1 Tbs.	flour
1 tsp.	baking powder

• *Toffee Sauce*

½ c.	unsalted butter
½ c.	heavy cream
1 c.	light brown sugar, packed
1 c.	whipping cream (optional)

Preheat oven to 350°F. Butter a 10-inch round or 9 x 9-inch square baking dish. Chop dates, add to a medium bowl with baking soda, and cover with boiling water. Set aside. With electric mixer, beat butter and sugar until creamy. Add egg and vanilla; beat until smooth. Combine flour and baking powder and gradually add to butter mixture. Stir in date mixture, and blend well with spoon. Pour into prepared pan and bake for 35–40 minutes.

When ready to serve, combine toffee sauce ingredients in a heavy-bottomed saucepan and boil gently for 8–10 minutes, until slightly thickened.

To serve, put pudding in individual bowls. Pour sauce over pudding, and top with fresh whipped cream, if desired. Serves 6–8.

• • • • • • • • • • Whitney Capps • • • • • • • • •
Proverbs 31 Ministries

There are so many great moments in life to celebrate, but perhaps none are more singularly significant than salvation. So when our firstborn, Cooper, asked Jesus to be his Savior, my husband Chad and I wanted that moment to be sealed in his memory forever. We decided to throw a rebirth-day party of sorts. It was important to us, however, that the celebration not be so much about Cooper but about the work God was doing in his life. So we threw him a "Yeah God" party. We invited both sets of grandparents over, who presented him with personal notes of encouragement and joy. They each read their letters to him; it was a priceless encounter. Chad and I also presented Cooper with his first "grown-up" Bible. It was a simple but sincere celebration of a life-changing experience. We have since celebrated with our second son, Dylan, at his "Yeah God" party. Our three-year-old, though unaware of the significance of the moment, already talks about getting his first Bible at his own "Yeah God" party. It's only a moment, but we want them to know how expectantly we waited and how exuberantly we ALL celebrate their new birth!

4

Ways to Stay Connected

Our hearts hunger to know that someone sees us, understands us, cares about us, and is praying for us. No one is too old, too young, too cool, too busy, or too far away to need a touch of love. In this section, we've got some ways to stay connected with those we care about.

As children get older, we need to get creative with how we connect. Our friend Melissa told us that she used to pray every morning over her children. But as schedules got busy, some mornings she might not even see her children. So she started to text them prayers and Bible verses. While she doesn't always get a response, she knows they love to hear from her. Her creativity challenges us!

THE ART OF NOTE WRITING

Although we love our texts and emails, nothing compares to a handwritten note . . . something we can tuck in a memory box and reread days, months, even years later, when our hearts need a reminder. The curve of Grandma's *L*, the way she wrote her *I*, and a distinctive signature . . . just a glance at familiar handwriting brings back memories. It's a treasure, especially when the one who wrote the words is gone.

A handwritten note is a gift that lasts. Not only will they love it now, they will treasure it in years to come. Not sure who might like one? Try *everyone*. Let's start with those closest to you.

CHILDREN

Children love a surprise note—even from Mom. It doesn't have to be fancy, just from the heart. It could be a joke or a quote, a question or a comment. The fact that you thought of them brings a smile. Stick a note in a lunch box, backpack, or gym bag. Write it with pen, pencil, or crayon. Don't second-guess yourself, just do it.

> **Write it on your heart that every day is the best day in the year.**
>
> ~ *Ralph Waldo Emerson*

Sheila S. told us she puts a note in her daughter's lunch box every day. On one side she writes a fun fact about the current season, an upcoming holiday, or a topic relevant to her daughter's studies. Sheila has also included facts about sports and history. Her goal is to spark discussion at her daughter's lunch table. But on the other side she writes a personal note, such as "Good luck on your test today," or "We love you." Sometimes this side also includes a short message from the family pet, just for fun.

Apparently, not only does her daughter enjoy the notes, but her friends do too. There was a week when Sheila fell behind and didn't think the cards would be missed. However, her daughter said she and her friends were wondering why she had not put any fun facts in her lunch that week. So the answer is yes, dear mother, they do care.

TEENS

Staying connected is a bit more complicated when children get older. Make sure the note can be read in private if your child is reserved. Tuck it in an envelope to be safe. And this might be the time to adopt a family code for those "special" messages.

Nancy V. shared a three-generation code her family uses to say, "I love you." It's so simple, but powerful. Her family uses the number 143: I = 1, love = 4, and you = 3. They sign it on cards, use it in text messages, and have even "said" it to each other across a room using their fingers.

The amazing thing is that Nancy's parents (who are in their seventies) started this when they were college sweethearts! They continued this code with Nancy and her siblings. And Nancy and her husband adopted it too. It's a three-generation gesture of love!

Karen

Ways to Connect for Family Love and Encouragement

I have known my husband, Todd, for thirty years and have been married to him for over twenty-seven. But I just found out a fact about him recently: he likes orange marmalade.

Todd had never mentioned it before. He'd been eating plenty of my homemade freezer jams for decades: strawberry, spiced peach, strawberry-banana, raspberry, even strawberry-rhubarb some years.

Never once did he reveal his love for the peel-laden, citrusy delight that is orange marmalade. But one day, the subject came up and he mentioned how much he enjoys it.

So for Christmas this year, in his stocking he got not only a jar of this confection, but a sleeve of English muffins to go with it—his favorite way to enjoy his beloved treat.

What little-known treat does your husband or loved one enjoy that they haven't tasted in years?

Do a little digging. And then?

Go out of your way to surprise them with some.

Next summer, along with mashing berries for my jam, I'll be trying my hand at home-canned orange marmalade.

It will be a new venture.

I'll have Smuckers on standby.

I just might need to call for backup.

COLLEGE BOUND

Glynnis

When my first son moved away to college, I had to get creative in how I communicated. The mom in me wanted to remind him of all the dangers he faced and to give him lots of motherly advice. However, the young man in him wanted to hear me say, "I trust you." After a rocky start, I stopped trying to coach him and started affirming his right decisions.

It wasn't so much the method of communication that mattered; it was what I said. My well-meaning advice communicated itself as distrust—and that was forging a chasm between us. Thankfully God showed me what was happening in time for me to change. Here are some simple tips to open communication with your college student:

1. *Funny texts.* Making them laugh is a great way to reduce college stress.

2. *Care packages* with a short note of encouragement. Tying encouragement with snacks is a winner.

3. If you are friends on Facebook, first *be thankful.* Lots of parents aren't. Then respect your child's space and keep messages private on Facebook. Especially if they already think you are a borderline stalker. Bring up concerns in person.

4. *Learn about new ways* to video chat like Google+ and Skype, or FaceTime on the iPhone.

5. *Be a source of grace, not judgment.* Your child might make decisions that aren't how you raised him or her. Here's your chance to model how God loves us and to make your faith attractive. Withhold snarky comments, and bless what is good and right. And increase your prayers.

6. *Create a written reminder* of your love and faith.

Donna came up with a wonderful way to continue to pour love and encouragement into her college-age children:

My daughter is a senior in high school this year and will be going to college four hours away from home in August. My son, who will be a junior in college, will be also leaving the nest to live on his own at the same time. So this past August (a year from the date they would both be leaving), I started writing them little notes and Scripture verses on index cards. My notes are to remind them how much they are loved by me and their dad, but most importantly, that the Lord loves them even more than we ever could. My prayer is the cards help remind them to stay focused on their salvation and on being servants for Christ no matter where they live.

Here's how the first card reads: "365 days from now you will be living on your own. Know that your dad and I love you but your Abba Father loves you even more than you can comprehend. He is always with you. John 3:16."

Donna A.

5

Reaching Out to Others in Hard Times

*W*hile most of this book is about celebrating the little things in life, sometimes it's right to set aside the celebration and share in someone's sorrow. In the midst of our busy lives, we need to take time to show love and compassion when others are going through a hard time. Here are a few ideas that touched our hearts. Let's take these ideas and expand them to include ministering to people in all kinds of pain.

When I started chemo treatment, my husband was unable to go with me. He was taking classes and also trying to be the only available parent to our two kids. I was too proud to ask anyone else to go with me. The first day, I remember getting hooked up, breathing fast and feeling completely helpless and alone. I then pulled out an envelope a friend gave me, simply labeled "Monday." Inside I found a card and a personal note. I did not let that card out of my hands that entire day. The next day I had a "Tuesday" card . . . and literally, I had a card for every day of treatment. Some sang, some made me laugh, some made me think, while others included small gifts. I even received a button that read, "Chemo sucks." I wore that thing out! Though my cancer is in remission now, I still have this huge stack of cards and remember how my friend took the time to be with me through these little, daily reminders . . . day after day and week after week. It kept me going. I really hope I have the opportunity to do that for someone else.

Bethany B. 49

August is a hard month for my mother-in-law, as it is the month of her husband's death anniversary, their wedding anniversary, and other things that make the absence of my father-in-law exceptionally hard. So two years ago I took a large desk calendar and tore out all the pages except August, and then decorated the calendar page with Scriptures, prayers, encouraging words, and stickers for each day, and called it her "Joy Month Calendar." It helped her get through the month and she's used it every August since.

Ayla S.

ON BEING NEIGHBORLY

Here are some simple ideas to take to your neighbors on a holiday or just when you think they need a pick-me-up.

Pumpkin Bread
(circa 1966)

Blend:

3½ c.	pumpkin puree
3½ c.	sugar
1 c.	oil
2	eggs

Mix well and add:

4 c.	all-purpose flour
1½ tsp.	cinnamon
1½ tsp.	salt
1 tsp.	cloves
½ tsp.	nutmeg
4 tsp.	baking soda

Bake at 350°F for 1 hour in two large, greased loaf pans until loaves test done. Cool 15 minutes. Flip out of pans. For frosting, mix together:

2 c.	powdered sugar
½ tsp.	vanilla

Thin with half-and-half or whole milk until frosting is thick but pourable. Drizzle over bread.

Chicken & Cheese Pot Pie

Old-fashioned comfort food makes a wonderful dinner for a family in need. And it is a snap to put together!

1 box	roll-out refrigerated pie crust
2½ c.	cooked chicken, chopped
1 c.	sharp cheddar cheese
1 (10¾ oz.) can	cream of chicken soup
1 (16 oz.) bag	frozen vegetables for soup (don't just use mixed vegetables, find one that includes potatoes)
	salt and pepper

Mix all ingredients except crust in a large bowl. Add salt and pepper to taste. (We use about 4 shakes of salt and 6–8 of pepper.) Roll out 1 crust in a pie pan, leaving the edges hanging over.

Place ingredients from bowl into crust. Roll out second crust on top. Use your fingers to crimp edges of both crusts tightly together to seal. (Push them in close to the pie so the edge of the pan still shows. This prevents the edges of the crust from burning.) Bake at 350°F for 1 hour or until crust is lightly golden.

Cinnamon Cappuccino Muffins

So easy and trendy. Delicious too!

• *Espresso Frosting*

6 oz.	cream cheese, softened
1 Tbs.	butter, softened
¾–1 c.	powdered sugar
½ tsp.	instant coffee granules
¼ tsp.	almond extract
¼ c.	miniature semisweet chocolate chips

• *Muffins*

2 c.	all-purpose flour
¾ c.	sugar
2½ tsp.	baking powder
1 tsp.	cinnamon
¼ tsp.	nutmeg
½ tsp.	salt
1 c.	whole milk
2 Tbs.	instant coffee granules
½ c.	butter, melted
1	egg
1 tsp.	vanilla extract
¾ c.	cinnamon (or semisweet chocolate) chips

In a bowl, combine all frosting ingredients except chocolate chips and beat with an electric mixer until smooth. Adjust amount of sugar as needed until frosting is a spreadable consistency. Stir in chocolate chips and set aside.

For muffins: in a large bowl, combine flour, sugar, baking powder, cinnamon, nutmeg, and salt. In another bowl, combine milk and coffee granules, stirring until coffee is completely dissolved. Add melted butter, egg, and vanilla. Mix well. Stir into dry ingredients just until combined and then fold in cinnamon chips.

Fill paper-lined muffin cups two-thirds full. Bake at 375°F for 17–20 minutes or until a toothpick inserted near the center comes out clean. Cool for 5 minutes before removing from pans to wire racks. Cool and frost. Makes 12–14 muffins.

Never worry about numbers. Help one person at a time, and always start with the person nearest you.

~ *Mother Teresa*

As we respond in obedience to God's leading, acts of kindness stir children's sensitivity and prime their hearts to be actively looking for ways to serve others in their family, neighborhood, and around the world.

· · · · · · · · · **Sharon Sloan** · · · · · · · ·

Proverbs 31 Ministries

Dear children, let us not love with words or speech but with actions and in truth.

1 John 3:18

As my husband and I spend these precious parenting years in the trenches, our desire is to train our children how to apply 1 John 3:18 and be mindful of the needs of those God has placed in our lives. We trust the Holy Spirit to gently nudge our children's hearts to action and to then fill them with the joy and peace that accompany obedience. All around us are opportunities to love with actions that bring honor to God.

When our children were small toddlers, I walked around our cul-de-sac with them in the mornings to bring newspapers from the bottom of neighbors' driveways up to their porches. On trash collection mornings, we often would bring the neighbors' empty trashcans up to their garage doors. Now, when our children see a newspaper or an empty trashcan, they often take action on their own. They are now tweens and can serve the Lord in useful and significant ways.

Don't let anyone look down on you because you are young, but set an example for believers in speech, in conduct, in love, in faith and in purity.

1 Timothy 4:12

PART 2

Holidays
through the Year

They celebrate your abundant goodness and joyfully sing of your righteousness.

Psalm 145:7

A quick flip through the calendar reveals holidays and holy days on every page. From New Year's Day to year's end, there are scores of occasions to gather with family and friends, throw a party, serve a feast, or toss confetti.

Although the entire family and some friends may join in on the festivities, often the work of planning, shopping, cooking, and cleanup will fall on your shoulders. To prevent becoming frazzled when pulling off these festive celebrations, you need simple solutions and creative ideas so you can spend less time controlling the chaos and more time creating memories.

This section will help you when it comes to those major (and minor) holidays of the year. How can you prepare and yet not wear yourself out? Are there shortcuts that might make the prep easier? What about activities to forge fond memories during these special times for your clan? And the food—the folks are going to need something to eat, and it would be oh-so-nice if it were something tasty that didn't break the bank or break your back getting it prepped and onto the table.

For all of this—and more—read on. And be sure to look for the many ways to sprinkle confetti as you celebrate. It's time to get our party clothes on. The holidays are waiting but we don't want our guests to be!

Are you ready? Then let the confetti fly. It's holiday time!

6

$\mathcal{W}$intertime Wonderment

New Year and New Beginnings

Because of the LORD's great love we are not consumed, for his compassions never fail. They are new every morning; great is your faithfulness.

Lamentations 3:22–23

INAUGURATE A NEW FAMILY CALENDAR

On New Year's Day, open a new wall calendar and lay out an assortment of new fine-tipped colored markers. Take turns entering special events, birthdays, anniversaries, holidays, graduations, and vacations on the calendar. Decorate these dates with hearts, flowers, and small drawings so that each one is personalized.

START A CHILDREN'S JOURNAL

A great way to capture your child's personality at every age is with a journal he or she keeps. Keep the journal handy and occasionally ask your child a question such as: What's your favorite animal? What are you thinking about today? If you could ask God one question, what would it be? Allow your child to write the answer in his or her own handwriting. If they are too young, then write the answer yourself exactly as it's dictated. This journal is a way to spend time together each day, and will be a treasured keepsake.

SET FAMILY RESOLUTIONS

Rather than making a long list of resolutions that are hard to keep, what are some simple things you can do as a family? Can you resolve to say grace before meals? Can you memorize one verse together each week? Can you take a walk on the weekend? Keep it easy and healthy. Working together to develop good habits provides accountability and some great family bonding.

A GOOD WORD

Karen

It is very popular these days to pick a one-word resolution for New Year's instead of making a long list of habits you wish to change. Last year, my daughter put a new twist on this concept. Instead of choosing one word for herself as a resolution, she picked one word for each member of our family as a prayer focus for that year. For one brother she chose "passion," and that year she prayed that this exuberant teen would have passion for the right things: trying hard in school, training harder for sports, growing his relationship with God. For me she picked "peace." She knew I was facing a lot of changes and even some sadness with some relationships that year, and she asked God to grant me His perfect peace daily.

Then, on Christmas Day, we each got a unique gift from her that illustrated her prayers. She made us each a photo frame by painting unfinished ones from the craft store. Then, with rub-on alphabet

> **Brothers and sisters, I do not consider myself yet to have taken hold of it. But one thing I do: Forgetting what is behind and straining toward what is ahead, I press on toward the goal to win the prize for which God has called me heavenward in Christ Jesus.**
>
> ~ *Philippians 3:13–14*

decals, she placed our individual word on our frame. In each frame she displayed a picture of her with the family member the frame was for. It was one of the most creative and heartfelt gift ideas I've ever seen!

NEW YEAR'S DAY OPEN HOUSE

Start a new tradition of a New Year's Day Open House. Start the year right by dedicating your home to the Lord and opening your doors to invite others in.

Keep the menu light and simple with finger foods, fresh fruit drinks, hot cider, and a dessert buffet.

Place index cards by the buffet and invite your guests to write a prayer request for the upcoming year. Commit as a family to pray over these requests.

FOOD FOR NEW YEAR'S DAY

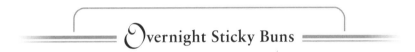

Overnight Sticky Buns

Prepare the night before and enjoy on a lazy morning with hot coffee and some parades!

½ c.	chopped pecans (or more if you like them)
18–20 sm.	frozen bread rolls
1 sm. box	butterscotch pudding, not instant
6 Tbs.	butter
½–¾ c.	brown sugar
¾ tsp.	cinnamon

Grease bottom of a Bundt pan. Sprinkle pecans evenly on the bottom. Place frozen rolls evenly on top of nuts. Sprinkle dry pudding mix over rolls. Melt butter in a small saucepan, add brown sugar and cinnamon, and stir until dissolved. Pour over rolls. Cover with a towel and set in oven overnight. In the morning, remove towel, heat oven to 350°F, and bake for 30 minutes. Invert on a platter and serve warm.

Note: These buns need approximately 12 hours of rising time.

Rumaki

2	boneless, skinless chicken breasts, cut into 1-inch pieces
¾ c.	sliced water chestnuts
12	bacon strips, cut in half
24	toothpicks

• *Marinade*

½ c.	soy sauce
3 Tbs.	brown sugar
1 tsp.	freshly grated ginger (or ½ tsp. ground ginger)
1	clove garlic, crushed
¼ c.	minced scallions
½ c.	water

Rumaki traditionally uses chicken liver, but this recipe makes it more appealing to all. This finger food will go fast, so make lots!

To assemble, take a piece of chicken and a piece of water chestnut and wrap them in a half slice of bacon. Secure with a toothpick and set in a baking dish. Repeat until ingredients are used up. Mix together all marinade ingredients and pour over rumaki. Cover. Refrigerate and allow to marinate overnight or at least several hours. To bake, drain the marinade and place rumaki on a greased cookie sheet. Broil until evenly cooked and browned, approximately 10 minutes. Watch and turn to avoid burning. Serve warm. Makes about 2 dozen appetizers.

Chutney Cheese Ball

16 oz.	cream cheese, softened
½ c.	mango chutney
¼ c.	green onions, chopped
1	clove garlic, minced
1 c.	Colby Jack cheese, shredded
	salt and pepper

1 c.   chopped pecans
        green apples, sliced
        crackers

Blend first four ingredients. Add cheese, and salt and pepper to taste. Form into a ball and roll in chopped pecans. Refrigerate until ready to serve. Put on a platter with sliced green apples and crackers.

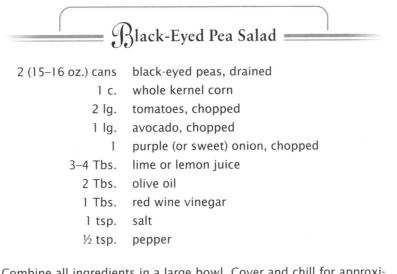

Black-Eyed Pea Salad

2 (15–16 oz.) cans   black-eyed peas, drained
           1 c.   whole kernel corn
          2 lg.   tomatoes, chopped
          1 lg.   avocado, chopped
             1   purple (or sweet) onion, chopped
        3–4 Tbs.   lime or lemon juice
         2 Tbs.   olive oil
         1 Tbs.   red wine vinegar
         1 tsp.   salt
         ½ tsp.   pepper

Combine all ingredients in a large bowl. Cover and chill for approximately an hour. Serves 6–8.

Monterey Chicken

This dish can be made ahead and refrigerated until ready to bake. It's easy to make and serve for a crowd.

         8 lg.   boneless, skinless chicken breasts
     1 (7 oz.) can   mild green chiles, chopped
          ½ lb.   Monterey Jack cheese, cut in strips
          ½ c.   dry bread crumbs
          ¼ c.   Parmesan cheese, shredded
        1–3 tsp.   chili powder (to your desired heat level)
         ½ tsp.   salt
         ½ tsp.   ground cumin

¼ tsp.	ground pepper
6 Tbs.	butter, melted

Rinse chicken breasts and pat dry. Cut a deep slit in the widest spot of each breast, and insert approximately one teaspoon of the green chiles and a cheese strip or two, depending on how thin you sliced it.

Combine the bread crumbs, Parmesan cheese, and seasonings in a shallow bowl. (A pie pan works great.) Melt the butter and put in another shallow pan. Dip each stuffed chicken breast in the butter, then coat in breadcrumb mixture. Place in a lightly greased baking dish. Repeat with remaining breasts. Drizzle with remaining butter.

Cover and chill for at least four hours for best results. (You can bake immediately, however.) Preheat oven to 400°F and bake for 25–40 minutes, until cooked through, depending on the thickness of your chicken breasts.

· · · · · · · · · · Backwards Day · · · · · · · · ·

Want to mix things up a little when the winter blues are threatening to settle in? Then celebrate Backwards Day on January 31.

This is an upside-down crazy day just for fun for the young and young at heart. Use your imagination.

Send text messages to your family members spelling all the words backwards.

Try your hand at writing letters backwards so that the recipient has to read the message by holding it up to a mirror.

Wear your shirt with the back in the front.

Eat your family supper that night starting with dessert and ending with the salad. What fun!

Walk backwards, or talk backwards.

Play a board game backwards, from the finish line to the start.

Are you starting to get the picture? This day is limited only by your imagination.

Wendy Blight

Proverbs 31 Ministries

New Year's Resolution

The first day of each New Year carries with it a myriad of emotions that often lead to promises and resolutions. We commit to lose weight, to exercise, to read our Bible, to be a better wife and mother, to eat better, or to pay off that car loan.

Oftentimes these promises and resolutions are grounded not on God but in self. We focus on the end result and not the process. The resolutions we make become things we check off our "to do" list. They do not bring profound, lasting life change.

A few years ago, I quit making New Year's resolutions. Instead, I wrote a prayer. Throughout the year, I watch in amazement as God works in my life and in the lives of others through my simple prayer.

I have written a sample prayer and invite you to use it as a model. Sit with the Lord and ask Him to help you personalize this prayer.

Father, I confess that I live a life that doesn't always honor You. My actions and my words do not reflect Your image. But I want to live a life that pleases You. Soften my heart to hear Your voice. Give me a hunger and a thirst for Your Word. Help me through Your Holy Spirit to listen and obey. Your Word says it is living and active, like a double-edged sword. Use it now to penetrate the deepest recesses in my heart.

Give me a heart that desires Your truth above all else. Give me a fresh filling of Your wisdom. Give me the strength to walk in Your truth, no matter the cost. Guard my heart. Keep my eyes fixed on You. Make me more like You. As I study Your Word, fill me and saturate me with more of You!

Today, Father, I surrender my life, thanking You that I am a new creation. Thank You for Your promise that You take all things and use them for Your good and the good of Your kingdom.

Direct my steps. I trust in You to do a mighty work in and through me this year and to carry it on to completion until the day I step into eternity with You.

Lord, I love You. Make my life a living testimony of Your love. I ask this in the powerful and mighty name of Your Son, Jesus Christ our Lord, who will do immeasurably more than we could ever ask or imagine. Amen.

· · · · · · · · · · · The Big Game · · · · · · · · · ·

Football season is wrapping up and TVs are tuned to everyone's favorite team! Rather than have the kids head one direction and the non-football-watcher another, try to create a family atmosphere where everyone can enjoy the day. If you have a houseful, consider setting up activity centers. Here are some ideas:

1. *Craft center.* Create a football-themed craft table. Bring magazines, scissors, construction paper, and stickers and have the kids create collages using the teams' colors.

2. *Creative center.* Have the kids divide into teams and create a cheer to perform during halftime. Have prizes for everyone.

3. *Cookie decorating center.* Make sugar cookies in football shapes and have a decorating table. With the right colors of frosting, of course!

4. *Puzzle center.* Find football trivia, crossword puzzles, or word searches and make them available.

5. *Face painting center.* Get team colors and paint streamers, mascots, and footballs on each others' faces. If you can find sports-themed temporary tattoos, add those too.

Oven-Roasted Asian Chicken Wings

3 lbs.	chicken wings
1 c.	soy sauce
1 c.	cider vinegar
½ c.	salad oil
7–10	cloves of garlic, crushed

Combine all ingredients and marinate chicken for several hours. Heat oven to 500°F. Line a large baking sheet with foil and spray with nonstick spray. Drain marinade from wings and place in pan in a single layer. Bake for 20 minutes. Turn wings and bake for another 10 minutes. Serve with ranch or blue cheese dressing and celery.

Nacho Bar

Place a big bowl of tortilla chips by the microwave and invite everyone to make their own nacho creation. Possible toppings include:

> browned ground beef with taco seasoning
>
> shredded, cooked chicken
>
> chorizo
>
> sliced olives
>
> sliced jalapeños or green chiles
>
> chopped onions
>
> chopped tomatoes
>
> queso dip (melt 1 lb. Velveeta cheese with either 1 can chili or 1 can Rotel tomatoes)
>
> shredded cheese (Colby Jack is ideal)
>
> salsa

If you choose shredded cheese, assemble your plate of nachos (minus fresh tomatoes and salsa), cover with a paper towel to avoid splatters, and microwave on high for 30 seconds at a time until cheese melts. Add tomatoes and salsa if desired.

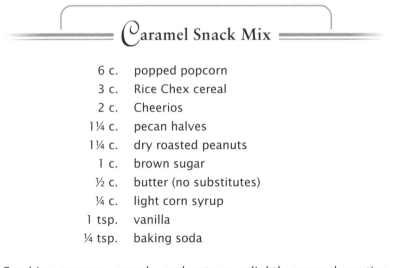

Caramel Snack Mix

6 c.	popped popcorn
3 c.	Rice Chex cereal
2 c.	Cheerios
1¼ c.	pecan halves
1¼ c.	dry roasted peanuts
1 c.	brown sugar
½ c.	butter (no substitutes)
¼ c.	light corn syrup
1 tsp.	vanilla
¼ tsp.	baking soda

Combine popcorn, cereals, and nuts on a lightly greased roasting pan. In a heavy-bottom saucepan, bring the brown sugar, butter, and corn syrup to a boil. Boil gently until candy thermometer reads 250°F. Remove from heat and stir in vanilla and baking soda. Immediately pour over popcorn mixture and stir to coat. Bake uncovered at 250°F for 1 hour, stirring every 10–15 minutes. Allow to cool before eating.

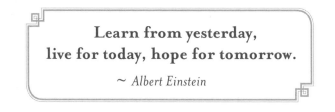

**Learn from yesterday,
live for today, hope for tomorrow.**

~ *Albert Einstein*

7

$\mathcal{F}$ebruary Festivities

• • • • • • • • • Black History Month • • • • • • • •

The roots of Black History Month go back to 1915, when Harvard-educated Dr. Carter G. Woodson and minister Jesse E. Moorland founded the Association for the Study of Negro Life and History (ASNLH). The ASNLH sponsored a national Negro History Week in 1926, and in 1976 President Gerald Ford declared February as Black History Month.

The ASNLH is now the Association for the Study of African American Life and History (ASALH), with a mission to "promote, research, preserve, interpret, and disseminate information about Black life, history, and culture to the global community" (http://asalh.org/aboutasalhmain.html).

The Library of Congress has created an amazing website specifically for what they call African-American History Month, www.africanamerican historymonth.gov. This site is filled with information about the rich and diverse history of African Americans.

Spend some time researching how African Americans have contributed to our society. Then pick one area to learn about as a family each year. Here are some suggestions:

Early Civil Rights Activists. Harriet Tubman, Sojourner Truth, Frederick Douglass, Mum Bett

Military Service. Tuskegee Airmen, Crispus Attucks

Authors. Phillis Wheatley, James Baldwin

Athletes. Jesse Owens, Althea Gibson

Inventors. Madame C. J. Walker, George Washington Carver, Garrett Morgan

Shrove Tuesday/Mardi Gras

Shrove Tuesday was the name given to the last day before Lent. *Shrove* means "to confess," and for Christians in the Middle Ages, it became known as a day of repentance. It also morphed into the last day to celebrate before entering into the forty days of Lent and abstention from something to share in Christ's sacrifice.

Shrove Tuesday is now known as Mardi Gras in many areas of the world, and has lost its significance as a day to repent. However, although many Christian churches no longer follow the historical church calendar, we believe any day to remember Christ and His sacrifice is important.

As the old saying goes, "It's more effective to light a candle than curse the darkness." And Romans 13:12 says, "The night is nearly over; the day is almost here. So let us put aside the deeds of darkness and put on the armor of light."

Perhaps your family can honor God on Mardi Gras and be that light in the darkness. Whether or not you recognize Lent, you can still prepare your heart for Christ's resurrection.

MARDI GRAS RECIPES

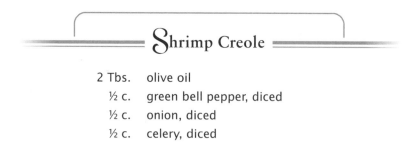

Shrimp Creole

2 Tbs.	olive oil
½ c.	green bell pepper, diced
½ c.	onion, diced
½ c.	celery, diced

1 tsp.	chili powder
1 (14 oz.) can	tomatoes
1 (8 oz.) can	tomato sauce
1 Tbs.	hot sauce
1 Tbs.	Worcestershire sauce
1 tsp.	white sugar
	salt and pepper
1½ lbs.	shrimp, peeled and deveined
	green onions, for garnish

Preheat slow cooker on high.

Heat olive oil in a frying pan, and add peppers, onions, and celery. Cook until softened. Add chili powder and sauté until caramelized. Remove from heat and pour into slow cooker. Add all remaining ingredients except shrimp.

Cover and cook for 3 hours on high. Add shrimp and cook for about 3 minutes, or until shrimp turn pink. Serve over rice. Top with chopped green onions.

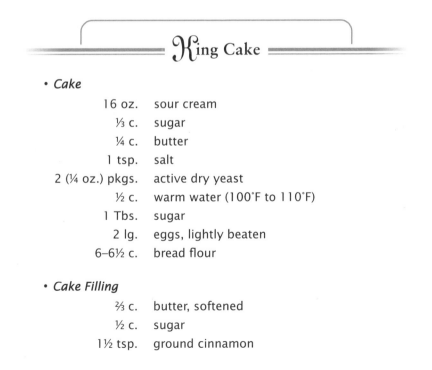

King Cake

• *Cake*

16 oz.	sour cream
⅓ c.	sugar
¼ c.	butter
1 tsp.	salt
2 (¼ oz.) pkgs.	active dry yeast
½ c.	warm water (100°F to 110°F)
1 Tbs.	sugar
2 lg.	eggs, lightly beaten
6–6½ c.	bread flour

• *Cake Filling*

⅔ c.	butter, softened
½ c.	sugar
1½ tsp.	ground cinnamon

• *Alternate Cake Fillings*

Blend together:

16 oz.	cream cheese, softened
¾ c.	sugar
1	egg
2 tsp.	vanilla extract

Or

2 cans	almond pastry filling

• *Glaze*

3 c.	powdered sugar
3 Tbs.	butter, melted
2 Tbs.	fresh lemon juice
¼ tsp.	vanilla extract
2–4 Tbs.	milk
	purple, green, and gold or yellow sugar sprinkles

For cake: warm sour cream, sugar, butter, and salt in a medium sauce-pan over low heat until butter melts. Allow to cool to 100°F. In a small bowl, stir together yeast, warm water, and sugar. Let stand 5 minutes.

Using electric mixer, beat sour cream mixture, yeast mixture, eggs, and 2 cups flour at medium speed until smooth. If using a stand mixer, reduce speed to low and gradually add enough remaining flour (4–4½ cups) until a soft dough forms. Otherwise, continue to mix flour in by hand until smooth.

Place dough on a lightly floured surface and knead until smooth (about 10 minutes). Place in a well-greased bowl, turning to grease all sides. Cover and let rise in a warm place until dough is doubled in size, approximately 1 hour.

When dough is risen, punch down and divide in half. Roll each half into a 22 x 12-inch rectangle. Spread ⅓ cup softened butter evenly on each piece, leaving a 1-inch border. Blend ½ cup sugar and cinnamon and sprinkle evenly over buttered dough. If you choose the cream cheese or almond paste filling, spread filling evenly across dough, using fingers or a spoon if necessary to spread.

Roll up each dough rectangle, starting at long side. Place one roll, seam side down, on a lightly greased baking sheet. Form dough into an oval ring and pinch ends together to seal. Repeat with second dough roll.

Cover and let rise again in a warm place until doubled. Bake at 375°F for 14–16 minutes or until golden brown. Transfer cakes to a cooling rack. Allow to cool approximately 10 minutes.

For glaze: blend first four ingredients, then add milk 1 tablespoon at a time until desired consistency is reached. Drizzle glaze evenly over warm cakes. While glaze is still moist, sprinkle with bands of colored sugars, alternating green, purple, and gold/yellow. Let cool completely.

Tradition says to insert a small plastic baby (Jesus) through a slit in the bottom once the cake is complete. Whoever gets the slice with the baby has to make the King Cake next year, or wins a small prize, like a cross to put by your bed to remind you to pray every night.

Valentine's Day

We love because he first loved us.

1 John 4:19

Valentine's Day is the perfect opportunity to share and show the love of Christ with your family, with those around you, and especially with those who have never experienced His love.

Here are some simple ideas for celebrating with your family and friends, and also some ideas for reaching out with the love of Christ to those who might be lonely at this time of year. And, of course, no section on Valentine's Day would be complete without a few decadent chocolate recipes!

ON LOVING AND LIVING

Here is a family idea for Valentine's Day to help bring the love chapter of the Bible—1 Corinthians 13—to life. Read through that chapter. Each time you see love described, write how it is described on a slip of paper. You should end up with phrases such as "patient," "kind," "does not envy," and "is not proud."

Place all of these slips of paper in a basket and leave it in a prominent place. On the days leading to Valentine's (count how many slips of paper you end up with, and start that many days before the holiday) take turns having a family member draw out a slip of paper.

Read the word or phrase. Then, as a family, have a time of prayer asking God to give you each the opportunity to display that particular characteristic of love to each other or someone else with whom your paths cross.

Gather back at dinner that night or just before bed. Share what you saw and learned. Did anyone have a chance to display godly love by exemplifying that characteristic? What happened?

SINGLED OUT

For many unmarried folks, Valentine's Day is known also as "Singles Awareness Day." They can feel left out of all the festivities and romance. You can help them to have a great day instead by intentionally doing something for them.

Have flowers delivered to their workplace.

Invite them over for dinner that night. You and your husband can always celebrate another day that week.

Write a handwritten sentiment telling them all the traits you love about them. Time the mailing of it so it reaches them on Valentine's Day.

Tell your husband you don't want a gift that year. Use the money to buy a single friend some fancy perfume or a pretty scarf.

Invite a whole group of singles over for dinner. Allow them to each make a side dish, and you provide the main dish. After dinner, play some board games.

Remember, Psalm 68:6 says, "God sets the lonely in families." Let Him set some in yours this year.

RED BREAKFAST

Glynnis

My friend Ginny W. hosts a special breakfast for her family every Valentine's Day with red as the color of the morning. Let your children help you plan this special menu beforehand. It might include fruit juice, strawberry-banana smoothies, cherries, and red velvet pancakes (see recipe below). Make sure to set the table the night before so you can enjoy a special breakfast without feeling rushed.

RECIPES FOR VALENTINE'S DAY

There are a few new traditions that I've started. We just did heart-shaped cinnamon rolls for Valentine's Day, but they were such a hit that I'm going to do them for birthdays and other special occasions too! I saw an idea to make heart cinnamon rolls from ready-made refrigerator ones by halfway unrolling each one and then rolling it back in. (You can do the same with a homemade recipe.) Apparently my son talked about it at school for two days.

Also, my son requests Lunchables for his lunches, but I've been making them for him to avoid the processed foods. Instead of cutting the cheese into squares and the ham into circles, I cut them both into hearts for Valentine's Day.

Stephanie C.

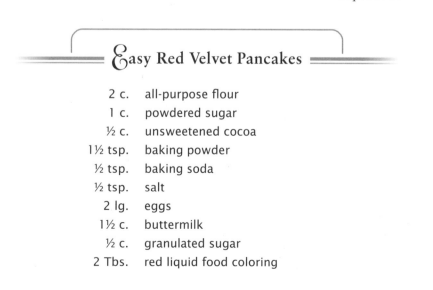

Easy Red Velvet Pancakes

2 c.	all-purpose flour
1 c.	powdered sugar
½ c.	unsweetened cocoa
1½ tsp.	baking powder
½ tsp.	baking soda
½ tsp.	salt
2 lg.	eggs
1½ c.	buttermilk
½ c.	granulated sugar
2 Tbs.	red liquid food coloring

Jesus replied: "Love
the Lord your God
with all your heart
and with all your soul
and with all your mind."
This is the first and
greatest commandment.
And the second is like
it: "Love your neighbor
as yourself."

~ Matthew 22:37–39

Stir first six ingredients together. In a separate bowl, mix eggs, buttermilk, and granulated sugar. Add to dry ingredients and blend until smooth. Stir in food coloring until blended. Heat griddle to medium high (if using an electric griddle, heat to 375°F). Brush melted butter or nonstick spray over griddle. Pour batter onto griddle in the desired size. Cook two to three minutes, or until tiny bubbles come to the surface. Flip and cook remaining side until golden brown. Serve with cream cheese topping, if desired. Serves 4–6.

• *Cream Cheese Topping*

4 oz.	cream cheese, softened
¼ c.	butter, softened
3 Tbs.	milk
2 c.	powdered sugar

To make topping, cream together the first three ingredients, then gradually add powdered sugar until desired consistency is reached.

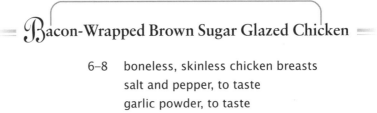

Bacon-Wrapped Brown Sugar Glazed Chicken

6–8	boneless, skinless chicken breasts
	salt and pepper, to taste
	garlic powder, to taste
	cajun seasoning, to taste (or your favorite seasoning blend)
6–8 strips	bacon
½ c.	brown sugar

Spray a 9 x 13 baking dish with nonstick spray. Rinse chicken breasts and pat dry. If the breasts are larger, consider cutting them in two pieces. Sprinkle salt, pepper, garlic powder, and Cajun seasoning on all sides of chicken. Wrap chicken pieces in bacon and place seam side down in baking dish. Cover each breast with a generous layer of brown sugar, patting it into the chicken. Bake at 400°F for approximately 25–30 minutes, or until the bacon is browned and chicken is cooked through. Spoon pan drippings over each serving.

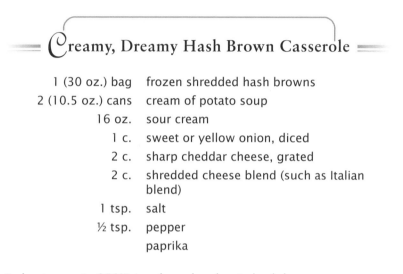

Creamy, Dreamy Hash Brown Casserole

1 (30 oz.) bag	frozen shredded hash browns
2 (10.5 oz.) cans	cream of potato soup
16 oz.	sour cream
1 c.	sweet or yellow onion, diced
2 c.	sharp cheddar cheese, grated
2 c.	shredded cheese blend (such as Italian blend)
1 tsp.	salt
½ tsp.	pepper
	paprika

Preheat oven to 350°F. In a large bowl, mix hash browns, soup, sour cream, onion, and cheddar cheese. Spread into a 9 x 13 or a 10 x 15 baking dish, top with cheese blend, and sprinkle salt, pepper, and paprika over the top. Bake for one hour or until casserole is bubbling and cheese is golden brown.

Oven-Roasted Asparagus

2 lbs.	fresh asparagus
	olive oil
	sea salt

Preheat oven to 350°F. Rinse asparagus and pat dry. Trim off woody white ends. Place in a glass baking dish and drizzle with olive oil. Toss to coat. Sprinkle with salt. Roast for 15–20 minutes, depending on the thickness of the asparagus. Watch to make sure it doesn't over-brown.

Chocolate Fondue

This easy-to-make dessert gets the entire family involved in the act of preparation. From slicing bananas to stacking marshmallows, kids of all ages can help.

• *Chocolate Fondue*

12 oz.	good chocolate (try dark), chopped
8 oz.	heavy cream
pinch	salt

Warm the cream until just below boiling. Remove from heat and stir in chopped chocolate and pinch of salt. Stir until chocolate melts and is well blended. Keep extra cream on hand to thin if necessary. If you have a fondue pot, pour chocolate into pot and serve over low heat. Or put in a small slow cooker on warm.

• *Suggested Dippers*

Use fondue forks or skewers to dip into chocolate.

bananas, sliced

strawberries

apples, sliced

large marshmallows

angel food or pound cake, cut into bite-size chunks

biscotti

pretzel sticks

brownie bites

Chocolate-Cherry Drop Cookies

These taste like a combination of chocolate-covered cherries and decadent fudge. Yum!

1½ c.	all-purpose flour
½ c.	cocoa powder
½ c.	butter (no substitutions)

1 c.	sugar
½ tsp.	salt
¼ tsp.	baking soda
¼ tsp.	baking powder
1	egg
1½ tsp.	real vanilla
1 (16 oz.) jar	maraschino cherries (reserve juice)

• *Frosting*

6 oz.	semisweet chocolate chips
½ c.	sweetened condensed milk
4 tsp.	cherry juice (from jar)

This recipe actually involves putting the frosting on the cookie before baking. To make frosting, melt chocolate chips. Add sweetened condensed milk and mix well. Add cherry juice and mix well again. Set aside. Combine flour and cocoa in a bowl. In another large bowl, cream butter, sugar, salt, soda, and baking powder until fluffy. Beat in egg and vanilla. Stir in flour mixture. Dough will be sticky. Drop by 1-inch balls onto lightly greased cookie sheet. Push one cherry into the top of each ball and spoon 1 teaspoon of frosting over each. Bake at 350°F for 10–12 minutes. Do not over bake. Makes 2½ dozen cookies.

· · · · · · · · · · · Presidents' Day · · · · · · · · · ·

Presidents' Day, the third Monday in February, was declared a national holiday in 1885 to honor George Washington (b. February 22, 1732). However, many people now use it to honor Abraham Lincoln (b. February 12, 1809) as well.

Rather than just having a day with no mail service or school, take this opportunity to learn a bit more about one of our nation's presidents. Here are some ideas:

Research which presidents were born in your state.

Pick a president and read their biography.

Try to memorize the presidents in order. Then have a contest with your children to see who can say them all first.

Let your children create a trivia game about the presidents to try and stump the adults.

Visit a presidential library or homestead.

PRESIDENTS' DAY RECIPES

First to live in the White House, John and Abigail Adams opened the Executive Mansion to the public with a New Year's Day reception in 1801. On the menu that day was Floating Island, a delicious pudding with a yummy meringue "island."

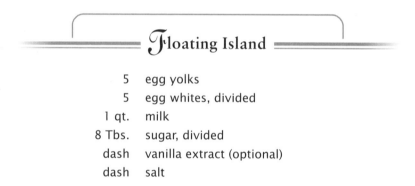

Floating Island

5	egg yolks
5	egg whites, divided
1 qt.	milk
8 Tbs.	sugar, divided
dash	vanilla extract (optional)
dash	salt

Beat egg yolks together with 1 egg white. Scald milk and stir a little into the egg mixture to prevent curdling, then add rest of milk and 5 tablespoons sugar. Cook over low heat until thickened. Remove from heat, cool, and flavor with vanilla if desired. Pour custard into bowl and chill. Add salt to remaining 4 egg whites and whip until soft peaks form, adding remaining 3 tablespoons sugar. Pour egg whites onto a shallow dish of boiling water to allow the meringue to steam-cook. When firm, drop by tablespoonfuls on top of the custard far enough apart that the "islands" do not

> **And so we know and rely on the love God has for us. God is love. Whoever lives in love lives in God, and God in them.**
>
> ~ *1 John 4:16*

touch. Serve cold. You may also pour custard into individual cups, dropping an "island" on top of each. Makes 6–8 servings.

Thomas Jefferson's Fricassee Chicken

3 lbs.	chicken pieces
1 tsp.	salt
½ tsp.	black pepper
½ tsp.	ground nutmeg
½ tsp.	paprika
2 Tbs.	olive oil
2 Tbs.	all-purpose flour
1 c.	water
½ c.	dry white wine (or chicken stock)
3 Tbs.	butter
1	small onion, chopped
6–8 oz.	small mushrooms, sliced
1 Tbs.	chopped fresh sage (1 tsp. dried)
1 Tbs.	chopped fresh parsley
½ c.	half-and-half
	hot cooked rice

Rinse chicken and pat dry. Sprinkle with salt, pepper, nutmeg, and paprika. Brown the chicken in hot olive oil over medium-high heat in a Dutch oven. Remove the chicken when lightly browned and set aside. Reduce heat, add flour to the oil in the pan, and stir constantly until light brown, 1–3 minutes. Whisk in water and wine/stock until smooth. Return chicken to the pan and bring to a boil. Cover and reduce heat to a simmer. Cook 50 minutes.

Remove chicken and set aside. Remove broth and reserve.

Melt butter in the Dutch oven, over medium heat, then add onion and mushrooms and cook until lightly browned. Stir in sage and parsley. Add broth and chicken back in to the pot. Stir in half-and-half. Cook over medium heat, stirring, until thoroughly heated. Do not boil. Serve over rice.

ℳamie Eisenhower's Million Dollar Fudge

Karen's mom used to rave about this recipe when she was a girl. She searched all over for it. If only there had been Google back then! Published by Time-Life in 1964.

4½ c.	sugar
pinch	salt
2 Tbs.	butter
1 (12 oz.) can	evaporated milk

Bring all ingredients to a boil over medium-high heat and maintain it for six minutes, stirring constantly. Do not burn.

In a large bowl combine:

12 oz.	semisweet chocolate chips
4 (1 oz.) squares	bitter chocolate
2 c.	marshmallow cream (or 2 7–oz. jars)
2 c.	pecans, chopped

Pour boiling syrup over chocolate and marshmallow cream, beating until melted and smooth. Stir in nuts. Pour into a buttered 11 x 16 jellyroll pan (a 9 x 13 pan will work too; the fudge will just be thicker). When fudge has cooled, cut into squares as desired.

8

Springtime Celebrations

St. Patrick's Day

May the strength of God pilot us, may the wisdom of God instruct us, may the hand of God protect us, may the word of God direct us. Be always ours this day and for evermore.

St. Patrick

Learning about St. Patrick and his desire to reach others with the good news of Christ is a gentle reminder of the difference one person can make in the course of history. Perhaps you will never be famous and have a colorful holiday named in your honor, but you can influence those with whom your life naturally intersects and help to point others to God.

He said to them, "Go into all the world and preach the gospel to all creation."

Mark 16:15

What do we really know of St. Patrick? Considering the way we celebrate St. Patrick's Day, you'd think it all had to do with shamrocks and leprechauns. But there is actually some wonderful truth that we can celebrate and pass along.

At about age sixteen, Patrick, a young Scottish man born into wealth sometime in the late fourth century, was captured by Irish raiders and forced into a life of slavery. He later escaped and was reunited with his family, but in a dream he felt called by God to go back to Ireland to spread Christianity. He preached the gospel and built churches throughout the country of his captivity until his death on March 17, 461. For the modern-day Irish, St. Patrick's Day is considered a time for spiritual renewal as they fondly remember the slave-turned-evangelist who spread Christianity to the Emerald Isle. Today we can use him as an example of what a young person sold out for God can do in their generation.

This St. Patrick's Day, we can change the way we think about this springtime holiday by asking ourselves a few questions: Do we have a desire to tell others about Christ and the awesome difference that He can make in their lives? Do we look for creative ways to bring the reality of Christ into our everyday conversations with those around us—especially those who do not have a relationship with Him? What are the things that attempt to hold us back from speaking naturally and freely about Jesus? How can we change this in order to be more effective communicators for Christ? And beyond what we say, what can we do that will speak louder than words? Remember, more is caught than is taught.

THE SHAMROCK

Legend has it that St. Patrick used the shamrock to teach others about the Trinity—the Father, Son, and Holy Spirit. He showed how the three different elements could exist in one entity. Irish Christians took to wearing the shamrock as a sign of their faith. Use a shamrock to talk to the young ones in your life about the Trinity, how God is present as three-in-one. For a fun treat once the Bible lesson is done, make and eat Irish Potato Pops!

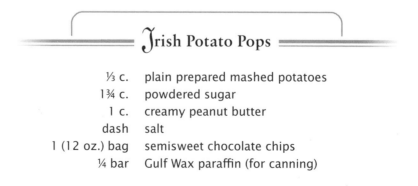

ℐrish Potato Pops

⅓ c.	plain prepared mashed potatoes
1¾ c.	powdered sugar
1 c.	creamy peanut butter
dash	salt
1 (12 oz.) bag	semisweet chocolate chips
¼ bar	Gulf Wax paraffin (for canning)

½ tsp.   vanilla
          chopped nuts, green sugar, multi-colored
          sprinkles, or coconut for garnish
          sucker or cake pop sticks

Mix mashed potatoes, sugar, peanut butter, and salt well. Roll in small
balls and place on large cookie sheet. Insert a stick into each ball. Chill
until firm. Melt semisweet chocolate and paraffin in double boiler over
very low heat. Stir in vanilla. Dip chilled balls in chocolate and roll in
chopped nuts or sprinkles. Place on waxed paper. Let set up and serve
at room temperature.

WEARIN' O' THE GREEN AND DANCIN' O' THE JIG

Gather your loved ones for a St. Patrick's Day celebration. Wear green.
Find out how to dance a jig on the internet. Crank up the Celtic tunes
and enjoy those you love. Here are some leprechaun-pleasing eats to make
your day a smashing success!

ST. PATRICK'S DAY RECIPES

Oatmeal Pancakes

This mix makes enough for several mornings' worth of pancakes.
Serve with warm maple syrup and hot bacon.

    3 c.   flour
    3½ tsp. baking powder
    ½ c.   sugar
    1½ tsp. salt
    1 c.   brown sugar
    1 c.   shortening
    3 c.   old-fashioned oats

To make mix, combine first five ingredients, and cut in shortening
until the shortening is mixed throughout. Add oats and stir. Store in
a large resealable bag.

To make pancakes, take 1½ c. of oat mixture and combine with 1 cup
water and 1 egg. Makes 6–7 small pancakes.

Easy Shepherd's Pie

2 lbs.	potatoes, peeled and cubed
2 Tbs.	cream cheese
1 lg.	egg
½ c.	milk
	salt and freshly ground black pepper
1 Tbs.	olive or vegetable oil
1 lb.	ground beef
1 lb.	ground lamb
1	carrot, peeled and chopped
1	onion, chopped
2 Tbs.	butter
2 Tbs.	all-purpose flour
1 c.	beef stock or broth
2 tsp.	Worcestershire sauce
1 c.	frozen mixed vegetables (corn, carrots, peas)
	butter and paprika

Boil potatoes in salted water until tender. Drain potatoes and add cream cheese, egg, and milk. Mash potatoes, mixing all ingredients together thoroughly, and set aside.

Brown beef and lamb in oil, seasoning with salt and pepper. Add chopped carrot and onion to the meat after a few minutes. Cook meat, carrots, and onion for about 5 minutes, stirring frequently. In a different pan, melt butter over low heat. Add flour and cook together about 2 minutes, until thickened and bubbly. Whisk in broth and Worcestershire sauce. Cook over medium heat, stirring constantly, until gravy thickens. Add gravy to meat mixture. Stir in frozen vegetables.

Heat oven to 375°F. Grease an 8 x 8 baking dish and fill with meat mixture. Spread mashed potatoes over meat. Top potatoes with pats of butter and a sprinkle of paprika. Bake for about 20 minutes or until top is lightly browned.

Irish Soda Muffins

A new take on a classic bread. Moist and delicious!

2 c.	all-purpose flour
3 Tbs.	sugar
1½ tsp.	baking powder
½ tsp.	baking soda
½ tsp.	salt
¼ c.	salted butter, chilled
1 c.	buttermilk
1 lg.	egg, beaten
¾ c.	currants

Preheat oven to 375°F. Spray muffin tin with nonstick spray.

In a large bowl, mix together flour, sugar, baking powder, baking soda, and salt. With pastry blender, incorporate butter until mixture resembles coarse crumbs. In another bowl, stir together buttermilk and egg until blended. Add buttermilk mixture to dry ingredients and stir to combine. Stir in currants.

Pour batter into muffin cups. Bake 20–25 minutes or until tester inserted in center comes out clean. Do not over bake.

Cool 5–10 minutes before removing muffins from tins. Serve warm or cool completely on wire racks before storing muffins in an airtight container at room temperature. Makes 12 muffins.

Triple-Layer Pistachio Bars

A sweet ending to your Irish meal. Serve with some Irish cream flavored coffee. *Erin Go Bragh!*

• *Crust*

1½ c.	all-purpose flour
¾ c.	butter (no substitutions)
¼ tsp.	salt
1 c.	pecans, chopped

Mix together all ingredients and pat into bottom of 9 x 13 baking dish. Bake at 375°F for 15 minutes and cool.

• *Cream Cheese Layer*

8 oz.	cream cheese, softened
1 c.	powdered sugar
1 c.	non-dairy whipped topping

Mix together cream cheese and sugar until well blended. Fold in whipped topping until smooth and then spread on cooled crust.

• *Pudding Layer*

2 sm. pkgs.	pistachio instant pudding
3 c.	whole milk
1 tsp.	vanilla

Mix together the pudding, milk, and vanilla; beat to pudding consistency and then spread over cream cheese layer. Cover and refrigerate 4 hours or more. Cut in squares to serve. Top individual pieces with an extra dollop of whipped topping before serving and sprinkle with additional chopped pecans if desired.

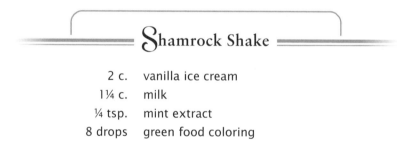

Shamrock Shake

2 c.	vanilla ice cream
1¼ c.	milk
¼ tsp.	mint extract
8 drops	green food coloring

Combine all ingredients and blend until smooth. Makes 2 12-oz. shakes.

Passover: Then and Now

Passover is the most important holiday in the Jewish faith. Although it isn't a part of most Christian traditions, it is a part of our history through adoption. Ephesians 1:4–5 says, "For he chose us in him before the creation of the world to be holy and blameless in his sight. In love he predestined us for adoption to sonship through Jesus Christ, in accordance with his pleasure and will." There is something beautiful about connecting our faith with the faith of God-followers thousands of years ago. So take some time to remember what God did for His chosen people.

Passover commemorates the Jews' deliverance from slavery in Egypt over three thousand years ago. The story starts with God speaking to Moses in the form of a burning bush. Moses was sent to Pharaoh to demand the release of God's people. Pharaoh refused. So God sent ten plagues to get Pharaoh's attention. The last one involved the angel of death passing over all the homes in Egypt and taking the life of the first-born of every family. The Hebrews protected themselves by marking their homes with the blood of a lamb. The symbolism of our spiritual freedom through the shedding of Jesus's blood, the perfect "lamb," is clear.

Jewish families remember the Passover every year with a ceremonial feast called Seder. Each course of the meal has deep meaning and turns the hearts of those participating toward God.

This year, consider hosting your own Seder meal. Research the components, purchase them as a family, and talk about God's miracles while you share them together. Take time to discuss how you have seen God provide for your family in the past year. When you host your Seder, be sure to set an extra place at the table. Modern-day Jews do this for Elijah. They even go looking for him during their time together. When they can't find him they declare, "Maybe next year." We, as Christ-followers, don't set a place for Elijah. We set one in anticipation of the coming Messiah, who will once again return to earth.

· · · · · · · · · · Spring Has Sprung · · · · · · · · · ·

March 21 ushers in the beginning of spring. For some, this means warmer weather. For others in a colder climate, it may just mean dreams of forthcoming balmy breezes. No matter your region, try some of these cheery ideas to spell spring at your place:

If the weather cooperates, make it a tradition to buy and fly a kite each year as a family on this day. If the weather permits, do it at a park and take along a picnic lunch. We've given you a menu plan and recipes below for a yummy one.

Plant flowers in pots for your porch each year on the first day of spring. The bright colors and lush foliage will help brighten up your home and invite the warm weather to come.

If you can't go on an outdoor picnic because no one told the cold weather that it is officially spring, don't fret! Spread a blanket on the living room floor. Don your best springtime apparel. Crank up the furnace if you must. Put on some sunny tunes and enjoy a picnic lunch.

Here are some recipes to get you started.

Waldorf Chicken Salad

• *Salad*

3 c.	cooked chicken, medium diced
¾ c.	walnuts, coarsely chopped
¾ c.	Granny Smith apples, diced small
½ c.	golden raisins
½ c.	celery, small diced
2	scallions, finely diced
	salt and pepper to taste

• *Dressing*

1 c.	mayonnaise
½ c.	sour cream
¼ c.	cider vinegar
1 Tbs.	honey

Combine the salad ingredients in a large bowl. In a smaller bowl, combine dressing ingredients. Pour dressing over salad and stir to blend. Please adjust the amount of dressing to your personal taste, as you might like less than this recipe makes. Serve with crisp lettuce and croissant rolls for a delicious treat. Makes about 6 cups of salad, enough for 6 large sandwiches or 8–10 smaller sandwiches.

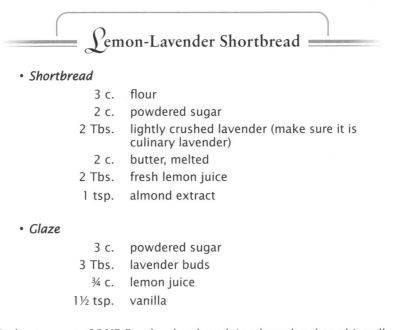

Lemon-Lavender Shortbread

• *Shortbread*

3 c.	flour
2 c.	powdered sugar
2 Tbs.	lightly crushed lavender (make sure it is culinary lavender)
2 c.	butter, melted
2 Tbs.	fresh lemon juice
1 tsp.	almond extract

• *Glaze*

3 c.	powdered sugar
3 Tbs.	lavender buds
¾ c.	lemon juice
1½ tsp.	vanilla

Preheat oven to 350°F. For the shortbread, in a large bowl combine all dry ingredients. Add melted butter, lemon juice, and almond extract, mixing until combined. Press the dough evenly in the bottom of a 9 x 13 pan with your fingers and score with a fork from one end to the other, creating shallow channels in the top of your shortbread.

Poke the shortbread with a fork about every 3–4 inches so it will not buckle while baking. Bake for about 25 minutes, or till the edges are lightly golden brown.

While still warm, slice into bars or squares. Place on wire cooling racks. Combine icing ingredients well and brush on individual pieces of shortbread. Once completely cooled, store covered at room temperature.

Tip: To keep the counter clean, place the cooling racks over wax paper to catch the icing drippings.

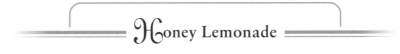

Honey Lemonade

⅓ c.	sugar
⅓ c.	honey
4 c.	water, divided
1 c.	fresh lemon juice

Combine sugar and honey in a small saucepan with 1 cup water. Heat, stirring, just until sugar dissolves. Let cool and pour into a pitcher. Add remaining water and lemon juice. Stir and refrigerate. Serve over ice with a slice of fresh lemon in each glass. Makes 5 8-oz. servings.

· · · · · · · · Good Friday and Easter · · · · · · · ·

GOOD FRIDAY

If your church family holds a special service on Good Friday, attending as a family is a wonderful way to commemorate the fact that Christ died for us. Here are a few other activities to help drive this point home:

- As a family (if all members are old enough to view the crucifixion scene), watch *The Jesus Film* by Campus Crusade for Christ or the movie *The Passion of the Christ*. Talk together and process your feelings after viewing it. What does it mean to you that Jesus died that cruel death for you?

- Make Good Friday a time to do some good deeds. Hang out at a coffee shop and randomly pay for another patron's drink. Or do the same at a gas station and pay to fill someone's tank.

- Make a main dish of lamb in honor of Jesus the Passover lamb. If your family isn't into lamb, buy a lamb mold and make a white cake with white frosting and coconut instead.

EASTER

Jesus said to her, "I am the resurrection and the life. The one who believes in me will live, even though they die."

John 11:25

Easter is the most treasured and important Christian holiday. On it, we celebrate the resurrection of our Lord from the grave. There is no better reason to pull out all the stops and celebrate BIG! Try some of these ideas to delight the young, teach about Jesus, and help the rest of us find hope and meaning in His triumph over death.

CREATE A HOPE BRACELET

Have you ever heard of the wordless book? It's the story of salvation without any printed words. History points to the great English preacher Charles Spurgeon as the creator of this simple idea: use black, red, and white to tell the gospel message. Black is for our sinful state, red for the shed blood of Jesus, and white for forgiveness of sin. Since that time, green has been added after white to reflect our spiritual growth after salvation, and gold has been added to represent heaven.

This Easter, make Hope Bracelets, which will give you the opportunity to tell the Good News of Jesus to all who comment on your bracelet. To make it, pick out beads in the five colors. For girls you might get fancy, and for boys keep it simple and masculine.

CHRISTMAS TO THE CROSS

Some families bridge the connection from Christmas to Easter by taking the trunk from their Christmas tree and forming it into a cross for Easter. If your family has a real tree, consider trimming off the branches this year and saving the trunk for next Easter.

Cut the trunk into two pieces with the top half being slightly smaller than the bottom half. Fashion the two pieces into a cross, tying it together with twine. Display your cross prominently as a reminder of Christ's sacrifice for us.

Put a stack of index cards in a pottery dish or woven basket by this rustic cross, and throughout the days leading up to Easter write what you are willing to sacrifice for the cross of Christ. Place each filled card back in the basket or punch a hole in the card, tie a loop using a red ribbon, and hang it from the branches of the cross.

Spring Cleaning: Home and Heart Edition

Are you old enough to remember spring cleaning? This was big in the 1970s when we were both growing up. An entire week or so was devoted to washing fingerprint-stained walls and woodwork, smudged windows, and grimy windowsills. Floors were mopped. Carpets were cleaned. Garages were overhauled and swept.

The calendar no longer reads 1970-something, but we can still devote some time when the warmer weather hits to doing some deep cleaning—of both home and heart.

For the Home

Now is the time to move furniture and vacuum and even shampoo the carpet if it needs it. This might also be the perfect time to rearrange the furniture in some rooms to spruce up the place and give it a new look.

Yes, wash windows and walls, but do it as a family and build in a little fun. Put on some upbeat music. Stop halfway for a family-favorite snack. Reward yourselves with a trip out for ice cream or a walk at a nature center or lovely park when you are done.

Have you wanted to repaint any rooms and give them a face-lift? With the warmer weather you'll be able to open windows to help with ventilation, so grab a brush and create a new look for your home.

Take this time to also spruce up your storage. Tackle one closet, cupboard, or dresser each day. Get rid of unwanted items by donating them or saving for an upcoming yard sale. Place back in the various storage areas only what you actually use and need.

What about your basement or garage storage? Now might be a great time to purge these often clutter-catching areas. Invest in storage shelves or large plastic bins to help reorder what you actually keep. With the rest—let it go! Someone else can surely use the "stuff" you aren't using. If donating to a charity store, be sure to get a receipt for tax purposes.

Are there moldy-oldies in your fridge? Ice sculptures in the freezer? Haul everything out and discard any outdated or no-longer-edible foods. Wipe down the insides or defrost the freezer if needed before re-stocking. Who knows what culinary treasures (or science projects!) you might find.

For the Heart

Create in me a clean heart, O God, and renew a right spirit within me.

Psalm 51:10 ESV

"Oh Jenny," I quipped to my friend. "You totally crack me up! All right then, we'll see you next week."

With that, the expectant mom grabbed her purse and her Bible, gave me a quick hug, and dashed out the door. She'd just announced to our Bible study group that her mother-in-law was coming to town for a few days and would be arriving later that night. Grandma was making the trip in order to assist her daughter-in-law in deep-cleaning her house. The nearly belly-busting mom was succumbing to what is fondly referred to as the "nesting urge," that instinctive compulsion moms have just prior to delivery or right before that wonderful trip to bring their waiting child home from the adoption agency.

What gave me a chuckle that fall afternoon was what Jenny was actually headed home to do before her hubby's mom came to town. Was it to prepare a hot supper or make room in a child's bedroom for Grandma's suitcase and such? Nope. Jenny was speeding home so she could do one thing: clean her house.

Yep, clean her house. Just *before* her housecleaning help arrived. She said she didn't want to be embarrassed by any killer dust bunnies or cowering cobwebs that just might be lurking somewhere Grandma might spy them. So she was going to "surface-shine" as much as she could before her mother-in-law pulled out the big guns . . . uh . . . er . . . vacuums and mops . . . to really tackle the hard-core deep-cleaning.

Perhaps we've all done something similar: flossed our teeth for the first time in months—right before our bi-annual hygienist's appointment at the dentist's office, or clipped our toenails and softened our heels—yep, the night before redeeming a pedicure coupon given to us as a birthday surprise from a friend. Something in us desperately doesn't want others to know just how dirty we actually let things get in our lives.

And this isn't just a matter of housecleaning and hygiene. We humans do this another way, and on a grander scale. An innate urge asserts we must somehow "clean up our act" before we can come to Jesus. We feel it when we meet Him for the first time. Our bulky baggage of sin burdens us down. So we try to "clean up our act" so we can then come to Him. But as contemplative, shepherd-turned-psalmist David declared in today's key verse, we need not attempt to spit-shine our own hearts, but rather must plead, "*Create in me a clean heart, O God.*"

Yes, *we* do the pleading. *He* does the cleaning.

Even those of us who have walked with Him for years sometimes surmise, when wading in the swamp of our sin, that we too must surface-clean the tarnish before He will ever want to use us again.

But just one action is needed: we must come to the Cleaner, the only spirit-sanitizer there is. And we must beckon Him, imploring our Savior to create in us a clean heart and renew our spirits so we may serve Him fully. Only then will the dust bunnies of darkness that oft-times shatter our souls be swept away completely so a renewed spirit can truly shine.

What a wonderful and spiritually effective way to be taken to the cleaners!

EASTER RECIPES

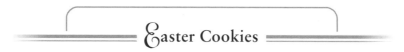

&aster Cookies

Tell the story of Easter using this simple recipe and Scripture. This should be done the night before Easter.

1 c.	pecans
1 tsp.	vinegar
3	egg whites
pinch	salt
1 c.	sugar
	resealable plastic bag (1 quart-size or 2 smaller)
	wooden spoon
	masking tape
	Bible

Preheat oven to 300°F. Put pecans into plastic bag, seal, and let the children break them into small pieces with a wooden spoon. Explain that after Jesus was arrested, the Roman soldiers beat him. Read John 19:1–3. Set the nuts aside.

Remove the cap from the vinegar and allow the children to smell it. Put vinegar into a mixing bowl. Explain that when Jesus was thirsty on the cross he was given vinegar to drink. Read John 19:28–30.

Add egg whites to vinegar. The eggs represent new life. Explain that Jesus gave his life so that we could live eternally with God and have a new life here on earth. Read John 10:10–11.

Sprinkle some salt into each child's hand. Let them taste it. Sprinkle a dash of salt into the bowl. Explain that the salt represents the salty tears shed by Jesus's followers. It also represents the bitterness of our own wrong choices. Read Luke 23:27.

Tell the children that there is a sweet part of the story. Add sugar to the bowl. Explain the best part of the story: Jesus died because He loves us. He wants us to know and belong to Him. Read Psalm 34:8 and John 3:16.

Beat with a mixer on high speed until stiff peaks are formed. Explain that the color white represents that God sees us as without sin thanks to Jesus's sacrifice. Read Isaiah 1:18.

Fold in the broken nuts. Drop by teaspoons onto a wax paper–covered cookie sheet. Explain that each spoonful represents the tomb where Jesus's body was put after he died. Read Matthew 27:57–60.

Put the cookie sheet in the oven, close the door, and turn the oven off. Give each child a piece of masking tape to "seal" the oven door. Explain that Jesus's tomb was sealed. Read Matthew 27:65–66.

Acknowledge that the children may feel sad to leave the cookies in the oven overnight. Jesus's followers were sad too when the tomb was sealed. Read John 16:20, 22.

On Easter morning, open the oven and give everyone a cookie. Point out the cracked surface and explain that on the first Easter Jesus's followers were amazed to find the tomb open. Now take a bite of the cookie. They are hollow! And the tomb was empty too because Jesus had risen! Read Matthew 28:1–9.

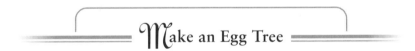

Make an Egg Tree

For an adorable decoration the whole family can make, try this idea for an egg tree. Here's what you'll need:

> small branches, painted white or left natural
> decorative pot filled with florist clay
> jelly beans
> multi-purpose white glue
> pastel plastic eggs
> pastel ribbon, ½-inch wide
> small Easter-themed items (small flowers, greenery, jelly beans, plastic lambs, bunnies, etc.) Just make sure they are small enough to fit in half an egg.

To create your tree, stick your branches into the florist clay. Arrange them so you have limbs to hang the eggs on. Cover the florist clay with a layer of glue, and spread jelly beans across the top to cover the clay.

Cut about 6–8 inches of ribbon for each egg. On one half of each egg, glue the ribbon to make a handle. Once you have made handles for all your eggs, allow them to dry thoroughly. Fill your eggs with tiny treasures, and hang on the tree.

ℬreakfast Bread Pudding
with *Warm Berry Sauce*

2	eggs
¾ c.	sugar
3 c.	low-fat milk
1 c.	heavy cream or half-and-half
½ c.	unsalted butter, melted
1 Tbs.	vanilla extract
¾ c.	raisins
½ tsp.	nutmeg
1 tsp.	cinnamon
8 oz.	stale French bread, cut in ½-inch slices

Combine eggs, sugar, milk, cream, melted butter, vanilla, raisins, nutmeg, and cinnamon. Pour over sliced bread in a large bowl, turning bread until it is saturated with the egg mixture. Allow to sit for 15–20 minutes.

Preheat oven to 350°F. Put bread in a buttered 9 x 13 baking dish; cover with remaining egg mixture. Bake uncovered for 45 minutes, until lightly browned and custard is set. Serve with warm berry sauce.

• *Warm Berry Sauce*

1 c.	fresh or frozen strawberries
1 c.	fresh or frozen raspberries
¼ c.	sugar
3 Tbs.	orange juice
1 Tbs.	lemon juice

Combine all ingredients in a saucepan over medium heat. Cook until the fruit begins to soften, about 5 minutes. Puree in a blender and return to saucepan. Keep warm until ready to serve.

Folded-Hand Prayer Pretzels

Often in the past, pretzels were a common fasting food during Lent. The shape of a traditional pretzel mimics the folding of hands in prayer. Make homemade pretzels as a family, and while they are baking, think of someone nearby who is in need of prayer. When the pretzels are done, enjoy some as a family and wrap up the rest to take to that person and let them know you are praying for them. If you make a big enough batch, you can take them to multiple people!

1 c.	very warm water
2 Tbs.	dry yeast (or 2 packets)
½ c. + 3 tsp.	honey, divided
½ c.	butter
1 Tbs.	salt
2½ c.	whole milk
8 c.	whole-wheat white flour (or unbleached flour)
	butter, melted
	coarse salt

In a large bowl, mix warm water, yeast, and 3 teaspoons honey. Let rest. In a large saucepan, melt butter. Add remaining honey, salt, and milk. Heat this to 120°F over medium heat (use a candy thermometer). Take off stove and let cool 10 minutes. Pour milk mixture into yeast mixture and stir well. Add flour 2 cups at a time. You may need to add a little more or less than 8 cups to make a slightly stiff dough. This depends on the humidity of the day.

Knead dough for 5–10 minutes. Place in a large, oiled bowl, cover, and let it rise for 1–1½ hours, until doubled in size.

Punch dough down to release air and knead on a lightly floured surface for 5 minutes. Take a piece of dough about the size of a tennis ball. Roll it into a rope about half an inch thick. Make it into a pretzel shape by crossing the ends, leaving about two inches on the ends. Then twist at the intersection of the two ends one time. Fold the ends down to touch the sides, creating a traditional pretzel shape. Repeat with remaining dough.

Place pretzels on a cookie sheet that has been lightly sprayed with cooking spray. Bake for 20 minutes at 350°F until golden brown. Do not over bake.

When you remove pretzels from the oven, brush them with additional melted butter, then sprinkle coarse salt on top. Serve plain or with mustard or sharp cheddar cheese spread. Enjoy!

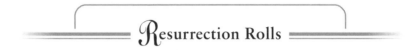

Resurrection Rolls

These rolls are a delicious way to tell the story of the Resurrection to children. Make them as an afternoon snack.

1 can	refrigerated jumbo crescent rolls
8	lg. marshmallows
2 Tbs.	butter, melted
3 Tbs.	sugar
3 tsp.	cinnamon

Preheat oven to temperature indicated on the package of crescent rolls. Divide the roll of dough along perforations into 8 triangles. Combine sugar and cinnamon and set aside.

Give each child a marshmallow, explaining that it will represent Jesus.

Have them dip their marshmallow into the melted butter and then roll in the cinnamon sugar mixture to coat. Explain how after Jesus died, two of his followers anointed his body with spices (John 19:40). The cinnamon sugar represents those spices.

Jesus's followers then put Jesus in a tomb (John 19:42). Have them place a marshmallow on the short side of each dough triangle. Tuck the sides up and roll down to the tip of triangle. Pinch the seams to seal. Each roll represents the tomb.

Place the rolls inside the oven and bake as directed on crescent roll package. Remove from oven and let cool. The marshmallows will have melted and disappeared during baking. Allow the children to break open the tomb (roll) and discover that the body of Jesus is no longer there. He has risen!

Spencer's Special Ham Glaze

An original from Karen's teenage son.

1 (12 oz.) can	Dr Pepper
⅓ c.	brown sugar
1 tsp.	garlic powder
½ tsp.	cinnamon
¼ tsp.	nutmeg

In a small saucepan, simmer all ingredients on medium-low heat until reduced down and thickened to the consistency of syrup. Brush on ham during the last 45 minutes of baking.

Manchego Mashed Potatoes

Manchego is a Spanish cheese made from sheep's milk. It's got a unique flavor, so try to find it for this dish. A good place to look for it is Trader Joe's.

4 lbs.	redskin or Yukon gold potatoes
4 Tbs.	butter, cut into small pieces
¾–1 c.	milk or cream
2 c.	Manchego cheese, shredded
	salt and pepper to taste

Scrub potatoes, quarter, and place in a deep pot. Cover with cold water. Bring water to a low boil and cook until tender, about 10–12 minutes. Drain potatoes and add back to the hot pot. Add butter, milk or cream, and cheese, and smash the potatoes to desired consistency. The cheese is slightly salty so taste before seasoning with salt and pepper.

Apricot-Glazed Carrots

1 lb.	baby carrots
2 Tbs.	water
¼ c.	apricot preserves

2 Tbs.	sugar
2 Tbs.	butter
¼ tsp.	salt
1 Tbs.	fresh parsley, minced

This microwave version saves oven space. Cook carrots in water in a covered microwave-safe bowl for 5–7 minutes or until tender. Drain. In another microwave-safe bowl, combine preserves, sugar, butter, and salt. Heat for 1–2 minutes, stirring to combine. Toss with carrots. Serve with fresh parsley.

For a crispier carrot, put blended preserve mixture and carrots in a frying pan and heat over medium until sauce is glossy and carrots slightly toasted.

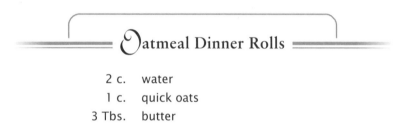

Oatmeal Dinner Rolls

2 c.	water
1 c.	quick oats
3 Tbs.	butter

Boil the above ingredients in a saucepan for 1 minute. Set aside.

In a large bowl, mix:

1 Tbs.	yeast (1 packet)
⅓ c.	warm water
1 Tbs.	sugar

Let stand for 3–5 minutes, then add:

| ⅓ c. | brown sugar |
| 1½ tsp. | salt |

Add oat mixture and mix well. Then add in 4¾–5¼ cups bread flour, just enough to make a slightly (but not overly) stiff dough. Turn into a lightly oiled large bowl. Cover and let rise until doubled, about 1–1½ hours. Punch down and separate into 3 balls of dough. Then, separate each of those into halves. Then take each half and separate into 3 equal pieces. The result should be 18 equal pieces. Roll each into a round ball. Place 9 rolls each into 2 greased round cake pans. Do so by placing 1 in the center and then place 8 more equidistant around the center. Cover with plastic wrap that has been sprayed with cooking spray to avoid sticking. Let rise 20–30 minutes, until sides of rolls begin to touch. Remove plastic wrap. Bake at 350°F for 20–25 minutes. Do not over brown. (Rolls can be covered with a piece of foil laid on top but not sealed to prevent them from browning too much.) Remove and cool. Serve with butter or homemade fruit jam. Yum!

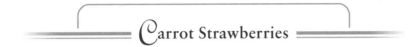

Carrot Strawberries

For a cute treat, surprise your family and turn some strawberries into carrots. Well, sort of. Melt some white chocolate chips in a double boiler. Immediately color orange using equal drops of red and yellow food coloring. Dip fresh strawberries in to coat, making sure to cover the whole berry, leaving only the green stem. Ta-da! Chunky carrots! *Note*: be sure the berries are completely dry before dipping.

Banana Macaroon Trifle

Add some wow factor by serving this delicious dessert in a clear glass goblet, topped with whipped cream and toasted coconut flakes.

2 Tbs.	butter or margarine, softened
1 c.	sugar
1	egg
¼ c.	milk
1 tsp.	vanilla extract
1 c.	sweetened flaked coconut
½ c.	old-fashioned oats
2 Tbs.	all-purpose flour
1 tsp.	baking powder
3–4 sm.	bananas, sliced
1 (4.6 oz.) pkg.	cook and serve vanilla pudding, prepared according to package directions
	whipped cream

To make the macaroon mixture, beat butter and sugar until well blended. Add egg, milk, and vanilla, mixing well. In a separate bowl, combine coconut, oats, flour, and baking powder. Stir in to liquid

• • • • • • • • Karen • • • • • • • •

A New Twist on an Age-Old Easter Tradition

During Lent, many Christians fast, giving up something they enjoy for forty days to observe the forty days Jesus prayed and fasted in the desert. It is a traditional way to prepare our hearts for Easter. Over the years, I've given up sweets, a particular television show, soda pop, and other assorted indulgences.

In recent years, however, I have stopped giving up something for Lent and, instead, I add something. Like serving in a soup kitchen once a week. Taking a hurting soul out for coffee every Saturday or acquiring a new habit like walking or reading the Bible *before* hopping on the computer.

Last year, I decided to take on writing a note of encouragement or thanks to someone each day of Lent. Forty notes in forty days.

In a way, I was still giving up something—my time, time when I could be doing something for myself but instead was doing something for another human. And I was giving up my money. Between notecards and postage, about $25.

What about you? Is there something you could take on for Lent this year?

mixture. Spread in a greased 9 x 13 baking pan and bake at 325°F for 25–30 minutes or until edges are golden brown. Allow to cool completely, then crumble. Set aside ¼ cup for topping.

To serve, spoon a layer of macaroons, a layer of sliced bananas, then pudding. Repeat and top with whipped cream. Serves 4.

Praise be to the God and Father of our Lord Jesus Christ! In his great mercy he has given us new birth into a living hope through the resurrection of Jesus Christ from the dead.

1 Peter 1:3

9

Other Spring Things

Tell a Story Day

April 27 is Tell a Story Day.

Glynnis

I grew up with stories. Every night my mother read aloud to me and my sister. While driving in the car, she told us stories of her childhood. We loved to hear them over and over, until we could tell them ourselves.

Stories resonate with us because God is the Author of the greatest story ever told. Psalm 145:7 says, "Everyone will share the story of your wonderful goodness; they will sing with joy about your righteousness" (NLT). And don't you love that we know it has a happy ending?

This April 27, celebrate Tell a Story Day with your own family. Here are some ways to do it:

Read stories from the Bible. If you aren't comfortable finding them yourself, check out a children's section of a Christian bookstore and invest in a Bible storybook. It's a great investment in your children's Christian education.

Tell your children a story from your childhood. Feel free to add some drama with your voice and gestures.

Check out an audiobook from the library and listen together.

Ask an older member of your family to tell about their childhood.

Retell an experience you had as a family.

Make up a story. Have someone start by saying a few lines, then pass the story on to the next person.

Play charades using book titles. Go on Amazon.com to find ideas.

Arbor Day

Arbor Day is the last Friday in April. However, some states choose a different day due to weather.

Although Arbor Day is not a Christian holiday, it is good for us to honor the Creator by caring for creation. Tending Eden was Adam's first assignment, and it has not been rescinded.

Here are some ways to honor God's creation:

Get involved in your local community's efforts to plant trees.

Plant a tree in your own yard.

Learn more about the local flora in your geographic region. Start by learning the names of the trees in your neighborhood.

Check out a nature guide from the library and go on a hike, identifying plants as you see them.

Choose to eat a vegetable- and fruit-based dinner to celebrate God's gift of nature.

Here is an example of a yummy vegetable-based menu complete with recipes. Enjoy!

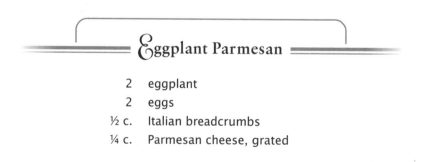

Eggplant Parmesan

2	eggplant
2	eggs
½ c.	Italian breadcrumbs
¼ c.	Parmesan cheese, grated

¼ tsp.	garlic powder
	vegetable oil
1 (26 oz.) jar	spaghetti sauce
2 c.	mozzarella cheese

Peel eggplant and slice ¼–⅓ inch thick. Sprinkle lightly with salt and allow to sit on paper towels while you prepare the breading.

In a shallow pan (pie pans work great) beat eggs. In another shallow pan, combine breadcrumbs, Parmesan cheese, and garlic powder. Dip each side of eggplant slices in beaten egg, then breadcrumb mixture, covering both sides. Heat a half-inch of oil in a heavy pan over medium-high heat. Fry a few slices at a time in oil until golden brown. Place on paper towels.

Layer slices in a lightly greased 9 x 13 pan, overlapping slightly. Cover in spaghetti sauce, sprinkle with mozzarella cheese, and bake in 350°F oven for 30 minutes or until cheese is melted and golden brown. Serves 4–6.

Chopped Vegetable Salad

To make this salad, choose your favorite vegetables and chop them into small pieces, including the lettuce. Mix the vegetables with your family's favorite dressing and serve! Here are some suggestions to make it colorful and crunchy.

1	head romaine lettuce
2	stalks celery
2	carrots
1	red bell pepper
1	cucumber
1	summer squash
¼ c.	sweet or red onion
½ c.	broccoli or cauliflower flowerets
½ c.	chopped tomato

Strawberry Rhubarb Crisp

| 2 lbs. | rhubarb stalks, sliced half-inch thick |
| 1¼ c. | sugar, divided |

1 lb.	strawberries, hulled and quartered
3 Tbs.	cornstarch
2 tsp.	fresh lemon juice
1 tsp.	pure vanilla extract

• Topping

½ c.	unsalted butter, softened
1½ c.	light brown sugar
1½ c.	all-purpose flour
1¼ c.	quick-cooking rolled oats
3 Tbs.	oil
1½ tsp.	cinnamon
¾ tsp.	salt

Combine the rhubarb and ¾ cup of sugar, stirring well. Let sit for 15 minutes. In another bowl, mix the strawberries with the remaining ½ cup sugar. Let sit for 10 minutes. Drain liquid from rhubarb and mix rhubarb with strawberries. In a small bowl, combine cornstarch, lemon juice, and vanilla. Add to fruit, mixing well. Pour mixture into a lightly buttered 9 x 13 baking pan.

To prepare topping, combine all ingredients in a medium bowl with a fork or pastry blender until mixture resembles large crumbs.

Sprinkle topping evenly over the fruit filling and bake uncovered for 30 minutes at 375°F. Reduce the oven temperature to 325°F and continue baking for about 30 minutes longer, or until top is lightly browned and fruit is bubbly.

Allow to sit 15–20 minutes before serving. Can be served with vanilla ice cream or whipped cream.

· · · · · · · · · · · · · · **May Day** · · · · · · · · · · · ·

Glynnis

The first day of May has been celebrated as May Day for hundreds of years. My mother remembers when she was a girl in the 1920s and '30s, she and her friends made sweet colored-paper cones from rolled paper and taped a handle to each cone. Then they filled the cones with fresh-cut wildflowers and hung them on the doorknobs of the homes of people they loved. In my mother's case, that was always her own mother.

What a lovely tradition this would be to deliver some fresh flowers to older ladies who might remember this tradition from their childhood. And start it anew with younger ones.

You can also make charming "vases" using cleaned soup cans with the labels removed. Cut a 1½-inch band of fabric to wrap around the can, and secure by tying a complementary ribbon around it. Punch two holes near the top and use more ribbon as a handle if you want to hang it as a surprise for someone you love.

Cinco de Mayo

While not Mexican Independence Day, as many mistakenly believe, May 5 has become a day to celebrate with our brothers and sisters to the south.

Cinco de Mayo is actually the day when the French were defeated at the battle of Pueblo in 1862. This victory kept the French from establishing a colony in Central America. Cinco de Mayo is the second most important holiday in Mexico after September 16, which is their Independence Day.

With Mexico being our neighbor, it's good to learn about their history. Check out a book from the library about Mexico and celebrate with a special dinner.

CINCO DE MAYO RECIPES

Glynnis

Growing up in Arizona, I was raised on Mexican-American influences. Here are some of my favorite recipes, adapted over years of trial and error.

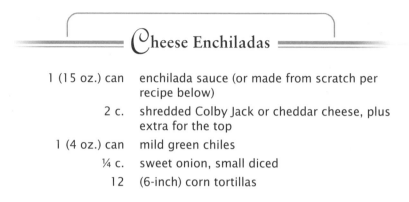

Cheese Enchiladas

1 (15 oz.) can	enchilada sauce (or made from scratch per recipe below)
2 c.	shredded Colby Jack or cheddar cheese, plus extra for the top
1 (4 oz.) can	mild green chiles
¼ c.	sweet onion, small diced
12	(6-inch) corn tortillas

Lightly grease a 9 x 13 baking pan. Spread a thin layer of enchilada sauce over the bottom of the pan. Mix cheese, chiles, and onion in a bowl. Warm 6 tortillas for 30 seconds in the microwave. Spread approximately 2 tablespoons of cheese mixture down the middle of one corn tortilla. Roll and place seam-side down in the pan. Repeat with the remaining 5 tortillas. Heat the other 6 tortillas and repeat stuffing and rolling. Pour enchilada sauce over all the tortillas, making sure they are covered. Spread additional cheese over the top. Bake at 350°F for 20 minutes, or until cheese is melted.

• *Homemade Enchilada Sauce*

¼ c.	vegetable oil
2 Tbs.	flour
2 Tbs.	mild chili powder
1 (8 oz.) can	tomato sauce
1½ c.	water
¼ tsp.	ground cumin
¼ tsp.	garlic powder
¼ tsp.	onion salt
	salt to taste

Heat oil in a skillet over medium-high heat. Stir in flour and chili powder, blending well. Reduce heat to medium and cook until lightly brown, stirring constantly.

In a small bowl, blend tomato sauce, water, cumin, garlic powder, and onion salt. Add to flour mixture and whisk until smooth. Cook over medium heat approximately 10 minutes, or until thickened slightly. Season to taste with salt.

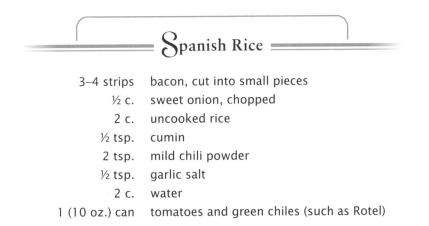

Spanish Rice

3–4 strips	bacon, cut into small pieces
½ c.	sweet onion, chopped
2 c.	uncooked rice
½ tsp.	cumin
2 tsp.	mild chili powder
½ tsp.	garlic salt
2 c.	water
1 (10 oz.) can	tomatoes and green chiles (such as Rotel)

Sauté bacon and onion together until bacon is cooked. Add rice, cumin, chili powder, and garlic salt. Stir and cook for 2–3 minutes until seasonings are well mixed with the rice. Add water and undrained tomatoes. Bring to a boil. Reduce heat to low, cover, and simmer for 20 minutes or until rice is done.

After you've made this once, you can adjust the seasoning to your family's tastes. One cup of salsa can be substituted for the tomatoes.

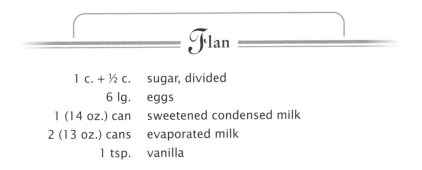

Flan

1 c. + ½ c.	sugar, divided
6 lg.	eggs
1 (14 oz.) can	sweetened condensed milk
2 (13 oz.) cans	evaporated milk
1 tsp.	vanilla

Preheat oven to 325°F. You can put the flan in individual custard cups or ramekins (6–8, depending on size), or an 8-inch square baking dish. You will also need a larger baking pan to put them in.

Heat 1 cup of sugar in saucepan over medium heat, stirring constantly, until sugar becomes caramel. Quickly pour approximately 2–3 tablespoons of caramel into each ramekin, tilting to swirl the caramel around the sides. Reheat caramel as needed.

Blend eggs together, then add both cans of milk, blending until smooth. Finally, blend in the remaining ½ cup sugar and vanilla.

Pour custard into caramel-lined ramekins. Place ramekins in a larger baking dish and fill baking dish with about 1–2 inches of hot water. Bake for 45 minutes or until knife inserted in center of flan comes out clean.

Remove ramekins from baking dish and let cool. When cool, store in refrigerator until ready to serve. Invert each ramekin onto a small plate, and the caramel sauce will flow over the custard.

· · · · · · · · · · · · · **Mother's Day** · · · · · · · · · · · ·

For you created my inmost being;
  you knit me together in my mother's womb.
                    Psalm 139:13

Each May we set aside one day to honor Mom and show her our love. And there's one thing on almost every mother's wish list: to be remembered by her children. The how doesn't matter all that much. A little effort goes a LONG way with Mom.

> **Her children arise and call her blessed.**
>
> ~ *Proverbs 31:28*

As you consider how to honor each mother in your life, keep in mind that what she wants more than anything is to know you love her. Here are some simple suggestions:

Arrange for a photography session at a local park. Moms love up-to-date photos.

Take her for a manicure and pedicure. Get one yourself.

Buy her a corsage to wear on Mother's Day. Tradition calls for a red rose if her mother is alive; a white rose if her mother has passed away.

Wash her car—inside and out.

Take her to the movies, and let her pick!

Write a poem about her. Get the entire family to help.

Plan a trip for just the two of you.

· · · · · · · · · **Karen** · · · · · · · ·

Other Mothers

I thank my God every time I remember you.
Philippians 1:3

While many use this time to thank the mothers and grandmothers in their lives, each May I like to also remember my "other mothers," women who touched my life, imparted their wisdom, and shaped my character.

Mrs. Esch lived across the street. Some in our neighborhood wrote me off, seeing only a latch-key kid from a broken home who was desperate for attention. Not Mrs. Esch. She looked deeper. She purposefully discovered my interests and learned all she could about them, even going so far as to join a softball team with me. She talked to me about what I wanted to do with my life someday. Most of all, she sensed in me an innate need to be introduced to the God who promises to be a Father to the fatherless. Soon after, she began to talk to me about "my calling," excitedly insisting she just **knew** God was going to use me in ministry one day. Thirty-one years later, she is now on my prayer team, the team that prays for me as I write and as I travel to speak. I thank my God every time I remember my mentor Mrs. Esch.

Think about your life. Who were (or are) your "other mothers"? The ones you thank God for every time you remember them? And what about the younger women in your life right now? Perhaps you are called to be an "other mother" to a soul who needs a little guidance on this side of heaven. You can give her a smile, a tender touch of grace, or a verbal "I believe in you!"

Women connecting with each other to encourage and dream create powerful partnerships.

Mother's Day is particularly painful for some, especially those who have lost a mother or a child. If you know a mother who is grieving, the best gift you can give her is to remember the one she has lost. A card, phone call, or text that says, "I miss her too," will let her know she's not alone in her sorrow. Consider giving a living gift she can enjoy, like a memorial rose bush.

SWEET GIFTS FOR MOM

I gave my stepson, Josh, an idea for a tradition to start with my wonderful daughter-in-law on Mother's Day. He traces my grandson Will's hand, then writes five things, one on each finger. The top of the homemade card says "I love Mom because . . ." On her first Mother's Day, Will was nine months old, so the things written on the fingers were phrases like "she makes great bottles" and "she holds my hand when I am trying to go to sleep." Year two was like, "she teaches me my ABCs" and "she introduced me to chocolate milk."

Since he's four now, he'll soon be writing on the traced fingers himself with a little help from his dad. I think it will not only be neat to see his hand grow but it will also be special to her to see how his wants and needs have changed from year to year, and to watch the cards go from her husband's handwriting to Will's. I SO hope Will is going to make these cards for his mom way into his adulthood. What mother wouldn't love that? I told Josh that now he needs to get her a nice mahogany box to start storing her cards.

Denise R.

MEMORIES FOR MOM

Karen

A few years back, I sat and pondered Mother's Day once again, not quite sure what to get my mom that year. Did she really need more perfume or another piece of jewelry? I wanted this year's gift to be unique, something only I could give her. So I gave her the gift of memories. It was the best present EVER! You can do this too. It is simple.

> **I remember my mother's prayers and they have always followed me. They have clung to me all my life.**
>
> ~ *Abraham Lincoln*

Just hop on the computer (or handwrite if you'd like—which may be even more special) and start listing your memories of your mother. They may be special. They may be silly. They might be of a holiday or a random day growing up.

Mine included her rocking me in our big, maple rocking chair when I had a fever. It is the same chair she rocked all of my babies in. I recalled her famous Jell-O—complete with celery and carrots—that I hated then but love now. I even listed how one day, on a dare from my brother and me, she strapped on my adjustable metal rollerskates and wheeled around the pool table in our basement, something totally out of character for my quiet and somewhat shy mom.

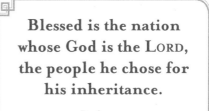

Blessed is the nation whose God is the Lord, the people he chose for his inheritance.

~ *Psalm 33:12*

I've also done this for my mother-in-law, only I had all five siblings and their spouses come up with memories for her too. Try to pick a nice round number, such as "Fifty-Nifty Memories of Mom." You can frame it and present it to her on Mother's Day or even on her birthday. She's sure to pull it out and read it again and again!

MOTHER'S DAY RECIPES

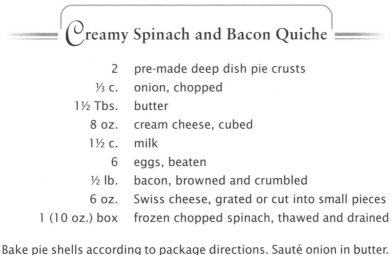

Creamy Spinach and Bacon Quiche

2	pre-made deep dish pie crusts
⅓ c.	onion, chopped
1½ Tbs.	butter
8 oz.	cream cheese, cubed
1½ c.	milk
6	eggs, beaten
½ lb.	bacon, browned and crumbled
6 oz.	Swiss cheese, grated or cut into small pieces
1 (10 oz.) box	frozen chopped spinach, thawed and drained

Bake pie shells according to package directions. Sauté onion in butter. Combine cream cheese and milk in saucepan over low heat, stirring constantly, until smooth. Remove from heat and gradually add to eggs, mixing until well blended. Add sautéed onions and remaining ingredients and mix well. Divide evenly between both shells and bake at 350°F for 35–40 minutes or until set. Allow to cool for 10 minutes before slicing.

Sunny Citrus Coconut Ice Box Cake

2 c.	sour cream
2 c.	sugar
¼ c.	orange juice
1 (14 oz.) pkg.	flaked coconut
1	white cake mix
1 (3 oz.) pkg.	orange gelatin
1 c.	water
⅓ c.	vegetable oil
2	eggs
2 (11 oz.) cans	mandarin oranges, well drained
1 c.	heavy whipping cream

Combine sour cream, sugar, orange juice, and coconut in a small bowl. Cover and place in the refrigerator. In medium bowl, combine cake mix, gelatin, water, oil, and eggs, mixing well.

Pour the cake batter into 2 greased and floured 9-inch round baking pans. Bake at 350°F for 30–35 minutes or until done in the center. Do not over bake. Cool for 15 minutes and then turn onto wire racks to cool completely.

Using a long, serrated knife, carefully split each cake into two horizontal layers. Set aside 1 cup of the coconut filling. Assemble layers as follows: first cake layer; one-third of the filling; one-third of the oranges; second cake layer; one-third of the filling; one-third of the oranges; third cake layer; one-third of the filling; one-third of the oranges; final cake layer. Refrigerate. In a large, chilled bowl, beat whipping cream until stiff peaks form; fold into reserved coconut filling. Frost the top and sides of cake. Sprinkle top with additional coconut. Store in the refrigerator.

Memorial Day

A hero is someone who has given his or her life to something bigger than oneself.

Joseph Campbell

On Memorial Day each year, celebrate the freedom we as believers have in Christ Jesus as we recognize the hand of God in our nation's history. Here are a few ideas to try.

Memorial Day honors those who died in service to our country. Contact a national cemetery in your city and see if they are hosting any services. Visit the cemetery as a family and bring small flags to place on graves. This act helps us remember that others gave their lives so we can enjoy the freedoms we have today.

Glynnis

My father was a Korean War veteran and was buried in the National Cemetery. Although he didn't die in battle, on Memorial Day we went to his grave, only to be surprised by the cars and motorcycles lined up as we approached. Flags flew and people waved as we gathered to honor the dead. It was a patriotic moment I will never forget, and made me appreciate my father even more.

> It cannot be emphasized too strongly or too often that this great nation was founded not by religionists, but by Christians; not on religions, but on the gospel of Jesus Christ. For that reason alone, people of other faiths have been afforded freedom of worship here.
>
> ~ *Patrick Henry*

Do you know someone who has lost a spouse or child in a war? Send them a card or give them a call at this time of year to let them know you are thinking of them, are still so sorry for their loss, and do not take lightly the price their loved one paid for our freedom. Better yet, if you live close enough, take them out for coffee or lunch. Offer to go with them to the cemetery to place flowers on the grave of their family member.

10

Sum, Sum, Summertime

· · · · · · · · · · · Best Friend's Day · · · · · · · · ·

June 8 is known as Best Friend's Day. Here are some fun ways to celebrate for young and old alike!

Share a lunch. You may take your child and their best friend out for lunch at a favorite eatery. Or pack a picnic and head to a park or beach. You could even plan to meet your own best friend if she lives nearby. For fun, pick a more expensive place you wouldn't normally go to and split a meal and the bill!

Share a memory. Does your best friend live far from you? Give her a call on this day to swap memories. Take a reminiscing stroll back in time and recall such things as how you met, the funniest laugh you shared, a time you got into mischief, or a time you were there for each other in sorrow.

Go on a hunt. Do you remember the name of your childhood best friend or another one from junior or senior high school? Try reconnecting with them by looking them up on Facebook or other places online. Send them a message on this day to reach out and make a connection with them again. It will be fun to see where you both ended up.

Jot a note and send a smile. If you live far away from a close friend you have known for years, pick out a favorite picture of the two of you together from years gone by. Place it in a simple frame or have it made into a mouse pad or mug. Handwrite a sentiment to go along with the fond memory. Mail it to them so it arrives near Best Friend's Day.

· · · · · · · · · · · · · · · · **Father's Day** · · · · · · · · · · · · · · ·

His preaching will turn the hearts of fathers to their children, and the hearts of children to their fathers.

Malachi 4:6 NLT

Take time to pamper the men in your life and show just how much you appreciate all they do for you, and remember this is a great time to celebrate both fathers and all the paternal role models in your life. Here are a few ideas:

No-chore week. Declare a no-chore week the week leading up to Father's Day. Everyone else mows the lawn, takes out the trash, or changes the light bulbs. Give Dad the time off to do whatever he wants to do. He might enjoy a free day to go bowling or simply relax in a hammock with a glass of iced tea.

Fill Dad's love tank. Tell Dad why you respect and appreciate him. Write your reasons on index cards, and in everyone's own handwriting. Then let Dad keep the cards with him to read when he needs some encouragement.

Watch a sporting event Dad likes. Put down the books, phones, or video games and actually watch the game with him. Just making the effort to learn about what he likes will make him feel loved.

Ask Dad about his work. Learn as much as you can about what he does so you can have more conversations in the coming weeks.

Video love notes. Make videos for Dad on your cell phone. Keep them short, but allow each child to say a message for Dad. Create your own love message, telling your husband what a great father he is. Send them as text messages the next week, spreading them out to keep the love going.

I love you because . . . Give a child some paper and coloring utensils and ask the question: Why do you love Daddy? Allow the child to draw or write their answers down. Tuck in an envelope for Dad to open as a surprise.

Dad's choice. As a family, rent and watch a movie but let Dad do the picking. And let Dad choose a snack to munch while watching.

Wherever he wants to go. Take an outing to a place Dad chooses. Perhaps it is a ball game or museum. Then stop at a park for a family picnic or swing by an ice cream shop for a big scoop of Dad's favorite.

Acronym of adoration. Have the kids write out Dad's full name across the top of a piece of posterboard. Then think of a word that describes Dad for each letter of his name and list it down from the letter on the board. For example: P A U L might be "Patient. Awesome. Unstoppable. Loving."

It's a party! Invite some other families over for a game of flag football or Frisbee. Serve subs, chips, and watermelon along with some lemonade. For dessert, set up your own county fair pie-tasting competition. Let the dads in attendance serve as judges and award the blue ribbon rosette.

All about Dad. Make Dad his favorite foods all day. If he likes pizza for breakfast then let him have pizza for breakfast. This day is all about Dad, so make sure meals are his favorites. If he doesn't have any favorites, here are a few dad-pleasing recipes.

> **As a father has compassion on his children, so the LORD has compassion on those who fear him.**
>
> ~ *Psalm 103:13*

Breakfast Pizza

1 (8 oz.) tube	refrigerated crescent rolls or pizza dough
1 lb.	bulk pork breakfast sausage
½ lb.	sliced mushrooms
½ c.	onion, chopped
1 c.	part-skim mozzarella cheese, shredded
1 c.	cheddar cheese, shredded

Roll out crescent rolls or pizza dough to desired size for crust. Bake at 350°F for 10 minutes. Meanwhile fry sausage, mushrooms, and onion until sausage is browned. Drain on paper towels. When crust is done, spread sausage mixture to edges. Cover with cheese. Bake at 350°F for 15 minutes, or until cheese melts.

Fruit Kabobs and Bananas Foster Dip

• *Assorted Fruit*

	strawberries
	green grapes
	pineapple chunks
	blueberries
	cantaloupe
	bananas
1 c.	banana yogurt
¼ tsp.	cinnamon
¼ tsp.	brown sugar
	wooden skewers

Cut fruit into 1-inch pieces and thread onto wooden skewers. Layer fruit in colors that appeal to you. For dip, mix cinnamon and brown sugar into the banana yogurt. Serve a few kabobs on Dad's plate with a pretty side cup of dip. Make as many or as few kabobs as you like! Dip will last for about 8 kabobs.

Two-Alarm Chili

2 lbs.	ground sirloin
4 med.	onions, diced
4–6 Tbs.	chili powder
1 tsp.	garlic powder (or 1 Tbs. fresh garlic, minced)
8 oz.	fresh or canned mushrooms, drained
1 (28 oz.) can	petite diced tomatoes
1 (28 oz.) can	tomato puree
1 (40 oz.) can	Brooks chili beans, mild

½ c.	ketchup
1 (4 oz.) can	mild green chiles, chopped (optional; it doesn't make it too hot)
1–2 Tbs.	sugar
	salt and pepper to taste

In a large pot, brown meat and onions with chili powder and garlic powder. Add remaining ingredients and simmer over low heat for at least an hour. Enjoy!

Pork Packets

For a simple and delicious grilling idea that doesn't make for a messy grill, try pork packets. Simply cut large squares of heavy-duty aluminum foil and spray with cooking spray. Place one boneless pork chop on the foil and top with 1 tablespoon soy sauce, 2 tablespoons cream of mushroom soup, and a few thinly sliced onions and green or red bell peppers. Seal foil and place on a grill over medium heat. Grill packets until pork is no longer pink—about 20–25 minutes (no need to turn). Serve with rice.

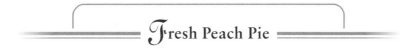

Fresh Peach Pie

No dad can resist this peach pie. Especially if you serve it *a la mode*!

1 box	roll-out refrigerated pie crust (or see recipe below)
5–6 c.	sliced fresh peaches
1 Tbs.	lemon juice
1 c.	sugar
½ tsp.	cinnamon
¼ tsp.	nutmeg
¼ tsp.	salt
2 Tbs.	flour
1 Tbs.	butter

Line pie plate with 1 crust. Mix all other ingredients except butter in a bowl. Pour into crust. Dot the top with butter. Cover with remaining pie crust. Crimp edges tightly, pushing toward pie and not leaving crust on the edge of the pan (this prevents burning), and prick all over with a fork. Bake at 425°F for 30–40 minutes, until bubbly.

- ### Blue-Ribbon from-Scratch Pie Crust

2 c.	unbleached flour
1 tsp.	salt
scant c.	butter-flavored shortening (about a tsp. or two less than a cup)
6–8 Tbs.	water from melting ice (seriously—cold tap water will not work as well, so get out a bowl, fill it with ice, and let it begin melting awhile before you begin)

Mix flour and salt. Cut in shortening with a pastry blender (or two forks if you don't have one). Stir water in lightly to form a ball. Do not handle too much! It will make the dough tough, not flaky. Divide dough in half and roll out one half on a well-floured counter to make a circle just a bit bigger in diameter than your pie pan. Repeat with top crust. Follow recipe for your favorite pie.

· · · · · · · · · · · · Mystery Day · · · · · · · · · ·

Anyone else have a hard time keeping the kids occupied and happy once summer hits? Last year I started a new tradition with my gang. I decided to host a "Summer Vacation Mystery Day!" We decided to make it an annual tradition. Here's how it worked.

I started our "Mystery Day morning" by giving the kids a fun poem that filled them in on what time to be ready and what to pack. We left at 9:00 a.m. and the kids had NO idea where we were going or what to expect! It was great!

I had different clues I had written ahead of time, and planned it so different people would give the kids the clues throughout the day. It was so much fun!

Our day included . . .

1. *Breakfast with Grandma.* You should have seen their eyes get huge when Grandma walked into the restaurant! She had a clue to get them to their next destination . . .

2. A visit to Mrs. N's. Mrs. N's clue let the kids know to get comfortable because we had a long drive to . . .

3. Michigan's Adventure water park! My kids had never been to this midwest theme park before—so they were beyond excited to be at this amazing place. What a blast!

4. Then some mystery guests showed up. The surprises continued when our good friend Julie and her daughter Berlyn met us there too. Woohoo!

The best part of my day was spending lots of quality time with my gang and fully enjoying our summer day. If you're looking for a fun way to add laughter, structure, and tons of memory making to your day, why not give the Mystery Day a try!

Cindy B.

· · Parades and Pondering, Fireworks and Food · ·

It is for freedom that Christ has set us free.

Galatians 5:1

Most Americans think of the Fourth of July as a time to perhaps catch a parade or fireworks and to throw something on the grill. If you are fortunate enough to be around a body of water, either natural or man-made, you might also take a dip to cool off for a while. But there is much more to this all-American holiday.

The Declaration of Independence was officially adopted by the Continental Congress on July 4, 1776. The drafting and signing of this important historical document launched the thirteen colonies on the path to freedom as an independent and sovereign nation. So today, when we celebrate, we are reveling in the freedom we have as a nation, freedom that has endured for over two and a quarter centuries!

Don't just go through the motions this year and fire up the grill as usual. Talk as a family about this day. Make up a quiz of little-known facts about July 4. (Did you know that archrivals John Adams and Thomas Jefferson both died on July 4, 1826?)

List the freedoms for which you are most thankful. Take the time to share your results with each other.

Take turns reading aloud Patrick Henry's famous speech, "Give Me Liberty or Give Me Death."

Watch a freedom- or Fourth of July–themed movie in the evening before you head out to the fireworks. Here are a few, along with their ratings. Be sure to research them online to determine if they fit well with your family's viewing guidelines. A great website for doing so is www.pluggedin.com.

Johnny Tremain (G) is a 1957 film made by Walt Disney Productions, based on the 1944 Newbery Medal–winning children's novel of the same name by Esther Forbes, retelling the story of the years in Boston, Massachusetts, prior to the outbreak of the American Revolution.

Miracle (PG) recounts a patriotically proud moment of the 1980 Olympics. Led by coach Herb Brooks, a group of rag-tag college guys brought about one of the biggest upsets in Olympic history, winning the gold medal in hockey over the Soviets.

> **Now the Lord is the Spirit, and where the Spirit of the Lord is, there is freedom.**
>
> ~ *2 Corinthians 3:17*

Rocky (PG, for some language). Fighter Rocky has a one-in-a-million shot at winning the fight on the Fourth of July. He decides to forget the odds and fight anyway. This movie might inspire you to run hard after your dreams in America, the land of opportunity. And you get to see Rocky's famous run up the steps of the Philadelphia Museum of Art.

Schoolhouse Rock: America (not rated, but suitable for all ages). Remember this Saturday morning cartoon with the catchy tunes? "We the people . . ." This fun-filled, animated feature is the perfect way to teach younger children about milestones and big events in American history.

BEYOND A BORING BARBEQUE

Of course this holiday is a perfect time to congregate with family and friends and enjoy some seasonal food. Here are some taste-tested favorites of ours.

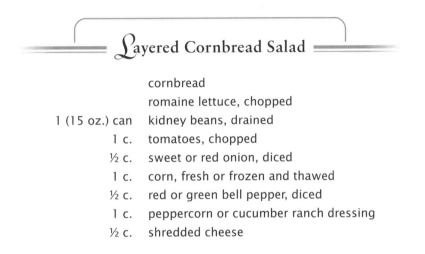

Layered Cornbread Salad

	cornbread
	romaine lettuce, chopped
1 (15 oz.) can	kidney beans, drained
1 c.	tomatoes, chopped
½ c.	sweet or red onion, diced
1 c.	corn, fresh or frozen and thawed
½ c.	red or green bell pepper, diced
1 c.	peppercorn or cucumber ranch dressing
½ c.	shredded cheese

Bake cornbread using your favorite mix or recipe. Allow to cool. Using a trifle dish, layer ingredients in order with cornbread on the bottom. Top with salad dressing and cheese. Serves 6–8.

Western Bacon Cheeseburgers

2 lbs.	hamburger
1 tsp.	seasoned salt
1 tsp.	brown sugar
6–12	frozen onion rings
12 strips	bacon
6	onion hamburger rolls
6	cheddar cheese slices
	BBQ sauce

Mix hamburger with seasoned salt and brown sugar. Form into 6 patties. Grill until cooked to desired doneness. In the meantime, fry bacon and bake onion rings according to package directions. To assemble, top each hamburger with cheese, BBQ sauce, 2 slices of bacon, and an onion ring or two. Serves 6.

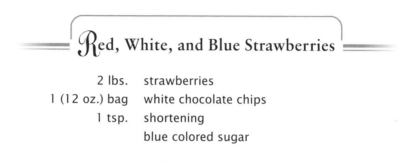

Red, White, and Blue Strawberries

2 lbs.	strawberries
1 (12 oz.) bag	white chocolate chips
1 tsp.	shortening
	blue colored sugar

Even the little ones can help make this oh-so-simple dessert. Wash strawberries and allow to dry well. Melt white chocolate chips and shortening in microwave, stirring every 30 seconds. When melted, dip strawberries in chocolate two-thirds of the way up, then dip in colored sugar one-third of the way. Set on wax paper to dry; put in the fridge to cool and harden. Makes approximately 20–30 strawberries, depending on their size.

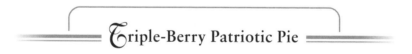

Triple-Berry Patriotic Pie

A red, white, and blue-ribbon winning pie Karen made for the county fair. Must top with vanilla ice cream for the color scheme to be complete!

• *Crust*

3 c.	all-purpose flour
1½ c.	butter-flavored shortening
1 tsp.	salt
1	egg
5 Tbs.	whole milk or cream
1 tsp.	vinegar

• *Filling*

2 c.	blueberries
2 c.	red raspberries
1 c.	blackberries

1 c.	sugar
5 Tbs.	cornstarch
1 tsp.	almond extract

Mix crust ingredients with a light touch until well blended. Roll out half the crust into a circle large enough for your pie pan on a well-floured surface. Place in pie pan. *Note*: you can also use a roll-out refrigerated crust to save time.

Mix filling ingredients and place in crust. Roll out remaining dough for the top crust and place on top of filling. Seal edges well and pinch to form edge of crust. Prick crust all over with a fork and bake at 350°F for 50–60 minutes, just until bubbly and crust is lightly golden.

· · · · · · · · · · · County Fair Party · · · · · · · · ·

Glynnis

During the summer it's hard to keep a small group going, but one year I hosted a county fair party to get our friends together, and it was a success! Together we planned the menu to include fair foods and created some simple games. Children and adults alike had fun.

Here's what our menu looked like:

Corn dogs

Watermelon

Funnel cakes

Deep-fried candy bars

Assorted old-fashioned sodas, served in a cooler filled with ice

Our games were simple things like a bean bag toss and making a bottle stand up using a string and a plastic ring. Other game ideas include a watermelon seed spitting contest, bubble blowing contest, and ring toss.

This simple, old-fashioned idea guarantees a screen-free experience, and is fun to plan and experience.

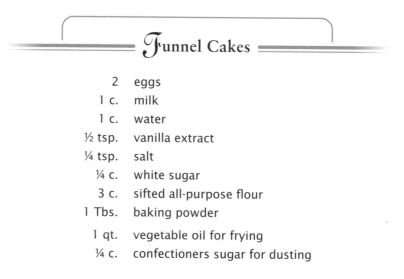

Funnel Cakes

2	eggs
1 c.	milk
1 c.	water
½ tsp.	vanilla extract
¼ tsp.	salt
¼ c.	white sugar
3 c.	sifted all-purpose flour
1 Tbs.	baking powder
1 qt.	vegetable oil for frying
¼ c.	confectioners sugar for dusting

Blend eggs, milk, water, and vanilla. Sift together salt, sugar, flour, and baking powder. Add to egg mixture and blend until smooth. Heat 1 inch of oil in a heavy frying pan to medium high heat, about 375°F. Using a ladle or measuring cup, pour ½ cup batter into hot oil in a circular motion. Fry 1–2 minutes until golden brown, then turn and repeat for other side. Drain on paper towels and dust with confectioners sugar while still warm. Eat immediately (just try not to)! Repeat with remaining batter, adding more oil and reheating as needed. Makes approximately 8 funnel cakes.

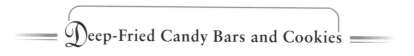

Deep-Fried Candy Bars and Cookies

	Assorted miniature candy bars
	Oreo cookies
1 c.	flour

You can use the funnel cake batter (recipe above) to coat your deep-fried treats. Put the candy bars/or cookies in the freezer for about an hour, unwrap, and dredge in flour before dipping in the batter. Fry until golden brown. Allow to cool slightly before eating.

Mom McComb's Lemon Ginger Balls

Karen

My favorite out-of-the-way eatery is a little retro place called Sweetie-licious Bakery Café. Its owner, Linda Hundt, was a cheerleader at a rival high school back when I also was cheering in the 1980s. (Don't worry; we are friends now!) Linda—a multiple national award-winning cook who has been featured on the Food Network and the *Today Show*—serves all sorts of family favorites that have been passed down through generations. This is a wonderful cookie that her sweet mama made all the time when Linda was growing up. To make them a little fresher, Linda added some lemon zest to the original recipe. They receive blue-ribbon raves every time! The secret to these—and all cookies, really—is to under bake them!

1 c.	sugar
¾ c.	shortening
1	egg
¼ c.	blackstrap molasses
1 tsp.	lemon zest
2 c.	flour
2 tsp.	baking soda
1¼ tsp.	cinnamon
1¼ tsp.	ginger
pinch	salt
	sugar

Cream sugar and shortening together. Add egg, molasses, and lemon zest, and mix well. Whisk together flour, baking soda, cinnamon, ginger, and salt, and add to creamed mixture. Mix together well, but do not over beat. Form dough into small balls and roll in additional raw or granulated sugar. Bake at 350°F for 8–11 minutes or until no longer doughy. Do NOT overbake.

· · · · · · · · · Camping/Vacations · · · · · · · ·

Glynnis

Before my husband and I had children, we led a youth group for seven years and we often took the kids camping or on retreats. The conversation always drifted to their experiences growing up, especially vacations or camping with their families. In spite of the inevitable troubles (sibling spats and Dad threatening to pull the car over), family trips were treasured in the hearts of these teens.

But why? Why would teens remember those times with such fondness? We believe the answer was that they had their parents' full attention. There were no distractions back then, no cell phones or laptops. Vacations were a time when parents enjoyed being with their children without interruption, and families created shared memories that last for years. The teens in our youth group didn't seem to care if it was a fancy Disney World vacation or a weekend trip to the mountains. It was their parents' invested time that mattered.

Right then, my husband and I decided family trips would be a priority. And now with our kids ages sixteen to twenty-two, they still are. We work year-round to plan for these times together, and they are investments of money and time that are solid and are reaping a harvest of strong family bonds today.

Tips for making vacations happen:

Start planning early. By planning a year ahead you can start saving and spread out the time it takes to plan. Do your research by buying travel books or visiting websites like www.TripAdvisor.com for ideas.

Make reservations as early as possible. Camping spots often open up a year in advance. Put this on your calendar and make your reservation the first day possible.

Make your own food. This is an obvious suggestion for camping, but we extend this to all family trips. We can eat peanut butter and jelly sandwiches for a week to enjoy the time together. Even that's part of the memories for our kids.

SIMPLE CAMPING FOOD

Breakfast: open-face bacon and cheese omelet. Cut bacon into half-inch pieces at home and store in resealable bag. Fry at campsite. When cooked through, add scrambled eggs and cook until desired doneness. Stir in shredded cheese for an easy one-dish meal. You can add onions and mushrooms to cook with the bacon if you like.

Lunch: Italian sub sandwiches. Bring an assortment of Italian meats, cheeses, Italian dressing, and hoagie rolls. Optional toppings include sliced olives, cucumbers, tomatoes, banana peppers, and lettuce.

Dinner: chicken kabobs. Cut chicken at home into one-inch cubes. Marinate using favorite marinade and store in a resealable bag. Double-bag chicken or store in a sealed container. Cut up vegetables such as zucchini, mushrooms, red bell pepper, and onion and store in separate resealable bag. At campsite, invite the family to make their own kabobs and grill. Add buttered French bread to complete the meal.

Dessert: Nutella banana s'mores. Make peanut butter cookies at home, and bring Nutella and bananas. Toast marshmallows over your campfire, and tuck between cookies spread with Nutella and thin slices of banana. Yum!

Book Lover's Day

August 9 is Book Lover's Day.

Did you have favorite books as a child? If so, this is the day to remember them. But we like to do more than remember the story or characters. We think books could be the foundation for a great theme for this day.

For example, let's say you love Jane Austen's *Pride and Prejudice*. On Book Lover's Day, establish a Jane Austen theme. This might mean you'd pull quotes from the book and tweet them. You might post photos of England on Facebook with a nod to Book Lover's Day. You might serve afternoon tea with scones. Are you very adventurous? Perhaps a Jane Austen–themed dinner.

Another book to celebrate would be *Cat in the Hat* by Dr. Seuss. Your day could start with green eggs and ham, and could progress to some fun in the house *a la* Thing One and Thing Two—without the destruction. Children would have fun memorizing pages and drawing a character.

If you are a book lover, your mind is already turning with ideas. Not only is this a unique "holiday," but it's a way to get your children invested in reading.

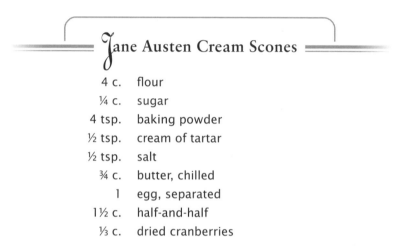

Jane Austen Cream Scones

4 c.	flour
¼ c.	sugar
4 tsp.	baking powder
½ tsp.	cream of tartar
½ tsp.	salt
¾ c.	butter, chilled
1	egg, separated
1½ c.	half-and-half
⅓ c.	dried cranberries

Preheat oven to 425°F. Mix all dry ingredients together. Cut butter into flour mixture until fine crumbs appear. Blend egg yolk into half-and-half. Pour into dry ingredients, mixing well. Knead dried cranberries into dough. Divide dough in half. Form into two rounds about 1–1½ inch thick. Score top of each round into eighths. Brush tops with egg white, sprinkle with additional sugar. Bake for 15–18 minutes. Serve with butter, fruit preserves, or lemon curd. And tea, of course.

Left-Hander's Day

August 13 is Left-Hander's Day.

Glynnis

It was hard being left-handed when I was growing up. Desks were specifically designed for right-handers with an armrest on the "wrong" side, there weren't left-handed scissors, and learning sports was a "watch me and do the opposite" sort of approach. Even learning to write was difficult, as we had to push the pencil, not pull it.

Most right-handers never understand the daily challenges of living in a world where things like scissors and baseball mitts and spiral notebooks are designed for them. Most left-handers simply learn how to adapt without much complaint.

If you have a lefty in your family, why not acknowledge their challenges and celebrate their differences on August 13? You can do so by having the rest of the family try to do things with their left hand. Try brushing your teeth, writing your name, and eating with your left hand.

· · · · · · · · · · · · · **Senior Citizens Day** · · · · · · · · · ·

In 1988, President Ronald Reagan made a proclamation establishing August 21 as Senior Citizens Day. President Reagan said, "For all they have achieved throughout life and for all they continue to accomplish, we owe older citizens our thanks and a heartfelt salute. We can best demonstrate our gratitude and esteem by making sure that our communities are good places in which to mature and grow older."[1]

Use August 21 as a reminder to honor the older adults in your life by recognizing and thanking them for their valuable contributions to your life.

Ask questions. One way to honor an older person is to ask them questions about their life. As a family, write down some questions you might like to have answered about where they grew up, what major events they remember, and what their favorite invention in their lifetime is. Then spend some time together sharing stories.

Show interest in an older person's life. This will bless them and teach your children that there's more to people than meets the eye.

1. Ronald Reagan, "Proclamation 5847—National Senior Citizens Day, 1988," August 19, 1988. http://www.reagan.utexas.edu/archives/speeches/1988/081988b.htm.

Help out. Many older people have a list of simple chores they can no longer do. It might be changing light bulbs or trimming bushes. Offer a few hours of manual labor as a way to say "thank you" for a lifetime of serving others. Set up a date in advance and ask for a list of chores and errands you can do. Bring a picnic lunch to share when you are done.

11

Autumn Activities

We remember before our God and Father your work produced
by faith, your labor prompted by love, and your endurance
inspired by hope in our Lord Jesus Christ.

1 Thessalonians 1:3

FIRST MONDAY IN SEPTEMBER

Labor Day is a day set aside to honor American workers and provide an
extra day to rest from their labors. This Labor Day, as we honor those
whose work makes our country strong, it's good to pause and remind
ourselves of God's view of work, and the value therein.

There's a tendency to think of work as a negative consequence of Adam
and Eve's sin. In Genesis 3, God told Adam that because of his disobedi-
ence, he would toil painfully in order to eat. But that's not the first refer-
ence to work.

In Genesis 2, after God created Adam and Eve, Scripture records, "The
LORD God took the man and put him in the Garden of Eden to work it
and take care of it" (v. 15). Work was Adam's first responsibility. In fact,
it would appear to be the first "call" of God on someone's life.

135

In our society, it's easy to devalue certain types of work as beneath us. But the Bible doesn't differentiate between jobs. In Scripture, all honest work has inherent value. Paul wrote the book of Colossians to the believers in Colossae, who consisted of men and women from all walks of life, including slaves. It was specifically to those slaves that Paul gave this word: "Whatever you do, work at it with all your heart, as working for the Lord, not for human masters, since you know that you will receive an inheritance from the Lord as a reward. It is the Lord Christ you are serving" (Col. 3:23–24).

> **All labor that uplifts humanity has dignity and importance and should be undertaken with painstaking excellence.**
>
> ~ *Martin Luther King Jr.*

Not only were those slaves likely responsible for the lowliest of tasks, but they were doing them against their will and with no hope of relief. In the midst of this undesirable situation, Paul reminds them that their work has value because they are working for Jesus. What an amazing paradigm shift!

In whatever work you do today, seek to find greater meaning in it. Work is not a punishment, but an opportunity to serve God with faithful diligence and a grateful heart. Even though you may not stay where you are forever, do your best today with dignity.

Here are some ways to celebrate Labor Day:

If you are employed by someone else, take the time to write them a thank-you note for trusting you with the work you have. Let your letter bless those in leadership above you.

Honor those who work on your church staff. People in these positions are servants, often working for below what they could make elsewhere in their field. It's also a hard job to do and stay positive. Gather a few other families to host a luncheon this week for your church staff. Write them notes of appreciation for their labor.

Work together as a family on a project. As you do, discuss the value of honest work. Talk through Colossians 3:23–24.

Put each family member's name in a hat and have everyone draw one at random. Throughout the day, seek to serve the other person. For example, you could make their bed or do their chore for the day. Work heartily for each other as if working for the Lord.

RECIPES FOR LABOR DAY

Since this is a day off for many, we've included one recipe that's a make-ahead so you can sleep in, and another recipe for the slow cooker. Enjoy the smells of this amazing spaghetti and meatball sauce cooking while you relax.

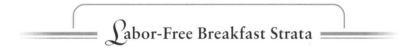

Labor-Free Breakfast Strata

Assemble this make-ahead breakfast delight the night before. In the morning, pull it out of the fridge and pop it in the oven to cook while you put your feet up! After all, it is Labor Day.

8	eggs
3 c.	whole milk
8 c.	French bread cubes (about ½–¾ inch cubes)
1 (10 oz.) box	frozen chopped spinach, thawed and squeezed dry
12 strips	cooked bacon, crumbled
1 c.	feta cheese, crumbled
2 c.	shredded sharp cheddar cheese, divided

Whisk eggs and milk. Add bread, mixing well. Add spinach, bacon, feta, and half the cheddar cheese. Pour into a greased 9 x 13 pan and top with remaining cheese. Seal with foil or plastic wrap and place in the fridge overnight. In the morning, remove and allow to stand at room temperature for 20 minutes. Bake uncovered at 350°F for 45–50 minutes or until lightly golden brown and puffy.

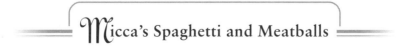

Micca's Spaghetti and Meatballs

Our friend Micca is a fabulous Southern cook. While you might not expect Italian meatballs from a Southern belle, trust us. This dish is amazing!

• Sauce

2 (28 oz.) cans	crushed tomatoes
1½ cans	water
1 (10 oz.) can	tomato paste
¾ tsp.	salt
¾ tsp.	pepper
¾ tsp.	garlic powder
2 tsp.	sugar
¼ c.	fresh parsley, chopped
2 Tbs.	oregano
1 Tbs.	basil
1½ c.	Parmesan cheese, shredded

• Meatballs

2 lbs.	hamburger
1 lb.	Italian sausage
¼ c.	fresh parsley, chopped
½ c.	Parmesan cheese, shredded
½ tsp.	salt
½ tsp.	pepper
½ tsp.	garlic powder
¼ c.	onion, chopped
2	eggs

Combine all sauce ingredients in a slow cooker or large pot. Combine all meatball ingredients and form into balls approximately 1½ inches in diameter. Put raw meatballs into the sauce and cook for 1½–2 hours over low heat. Remove the meatballs from the sauce and cook sauce another 2–3 hours. Return meatballs to sauce and warm. Serve over pasta.

Cheesy Bread

1 loaf	French bread
¼ c.	butter, melted
1 tsp.	garlic powder
1–2 c.	asiago or mozzarella cheese (or other Italian blend), shredded

Slice French bread lengthwise. Lay cut side up on a baking pan. Mix garlic powder with melted butter and spread over bread. Top with shredded cheese. Broil 1–3 minutes, watching carefully so it doesn't burn!

End of Garden Salsa

This is a great way to use up those last few veggies still growing in the garden.

6 med.	tomatoes, finely chopped
½ c.	green pepper, finely chopped
½ c.	onion, finely chopped
½ c.	red pepper, finely chopped
½ c.	cucumbers, chopped
⅓ c.	carrots, shredded
1 Tbs.	jalapeno pepper, minced
6 cloves	garlic, minced
2 Tbs.	fresh cilantro, chopped
1 Tbs.	cider vinegar
1 Tbs.	lemon juice
2 tsp.	olive oil
1 tsp.	salt

Combine all ingredients in a bowl and refrigerate at least two hours before serving. Serve with tortilla chips.

Grandparents Day

Grandparents Day is the first Sunday after Labor Day.

The Bible is clear that we are to honor our parents. In fact, it's one of the Ten Commandments. Proverbs 20:29 also honors our older generation, saying, "The glory of young men is their strength, gray hair the splendor of the old." On Grandparents Day, be intentional in honoring those who gave your parents life. These suggestions can be used for your grandparents or to help your children honor your parents.

Give a subscription to a genealogy website, with the promise to learn about the family tree together.

Interview your grandparents and write a biography. Two of my (Glynnis's) children had the same seventh grade teacher who assigned a biography as a book report. It needed to be the oldest living relative they knew. This meant my father for one and my mother for the other. This project took preparation on my children's part first as they created interview questions. Then there were several meetings together as they gathered photos and talked about the questions. I helped copy the photos and create the report . . . and I'm happy to say we (I mean they) both got an A.

> **She sets about her work vigorously; her arms are strong for her tasks. She sees that her trading is profitable, and her lamp does not go out at night.**
>
> ~ *Proverbs 31:17–18*

Create a spa day for Grandma. Give her a manicure, pedicure, and facial. She will love the physical touch.

Ask for stories about your mother or father. What were they like as a child? What did they excel in? Did they ever get in trouble?

Start a family cookbook. Ask your grandmother and grandfather to share their favorite recipes. If they don't have a written recipe, sit with them while they make your favorite dish, and capture it in writing. Continue to gather recipes and share them with your children.

RECIPES FOR GRANDPARENTS DAY

Go back in the family annals for favorite family recipes. Here's one each from Glynnis and Karen.

Karen

My grandma Elsie was famous for making anything with the abundance of blackberries that grew on their property in southern Indiana. My mother remembers canning over one hundred quarts each summer of the luscious fruit! Grandma Elsie's five kids especially loved her blackberry cobbler.

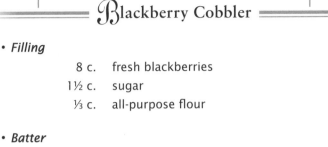

Blackberry Cobbler

- *Filling*

8 c.	fresh blackberries
1½ c.	sugar
⅓ c.	all-purpose flour

- *Batter*

2 c.	all-purpose flour
1 c.	sugar
1 Tbs.	baking powder
1 tsp.	salt
1½ c.	whole milk
½ c.	butter, melted

- *Topping*

1 c.	heavy cream
2–3 Tbs.	sugar
½ tsp.	vanilla extract

Preheat oven to 350°F. Lightly toss filling ingredients together and place in a buttered 9 x 13 pan. Mix batter ingredients until smooth and dollop over the berries, making sure there is batter all around the edges to prevent berries from boiling over. Bake on center rack in the oven for 60–75 minutes, until berries are bubbling and crust is no longer doughy. Whip cream with sugar and vanilla and serve on top of warm cobbler. Old-fashioned flavor!

Glynnis

My father's mother was a petite, roundish Welsh woman named Anna Mae Owens. My little sister and I would spend the night at her house and make mud pies to sell to her neighbors. She once told me lipstick was poisonous. It kept me out of her makeup and I wondered for years how she could wear it. Smelling these cookies hot from the oven takes me right back to her kitchen.

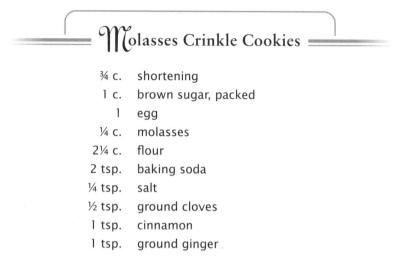

Molasses Crinkle Cookies

¾ c.	shortening
1 c.	brown sugar, packed
1	egg
¼ c.	molasses
2¼ c.	flour
2 tsp.	baking soda
¼ tsp.	salt
½ tsp.	ground cloves
1 tsp.	cinnamon
1 tsp.	ground ginger

Cream together shortening, sugar, egg, and molasses. In a separate bowl, combine dry ingredients. Mix together. Chill dough for about an hour. Heat oven to 375°F. Form dough into 1-inch balls. Dip top of each ball in sugar and place on ungreased cookie sheet. Sprinkle a drop of water on each cookie and lightly press down. Bake 10–12 minutes, until tops begin to crack.

Patriot Day

On September 11, 2002, President George W. Bush declared September 11 as Patriot Day. This is a day to remember and honor those who lost their lives in the attacks of September 11, 2001 in New York, Pennsylvania, and Washington, DC. Check in your area to see if there will be any ceremonies or services commemorating this day. Or, in honor of the first responders who lost their lives that day, take some goodies to your local fire or police station or hospital emergency room. You may want to check ahead to see if they can only accept store-bought treats. Or, instead of treats, drop off some gift cards to a local coffee shop or pizzeria.

Mexican Independence Day

While Cinco de Mayo is the better-known Mexican holiday, September 16 is actually Mexico's Independence Day. Around 6:00 a.m. on September 16, 1810, Miguel Hidalgo, a Spanish priest, declared independence from the Spanish crown and war against the government. This war would last until 1822, when Mexico finally gained control of its own government.

Use the day to learn about our neighbors to the south. We've included some recipes in the Cinco de Mayo section you can try. Or check out a Mexican cookbook from the library and try some on your own.

Johnny Appleseed Day

September 26 is Johnny Appleseed Day.

John Chapman, often called Johnny Appleseed, was born on September 26, 1774 in Leominster, Massachusetts. His father, Nathaniel Chapman, was a farmer and a soldier in the Revolutionary War. Sadly, John's mother died of tuberculosis during the war. When he was a boy, his father apprenticed him to a local apple orchard.

John took his knowledge and expanded the business to parts of Pennsylvania, Ohio, Indiana, Illinois, and the northern counties of present-day West Virginia, becoming an American legend in the process.

Remember Johnny Appleseed with apple-themed activities today. Visit an apple orchard as a family, and pick up some crisp apples for munching later.

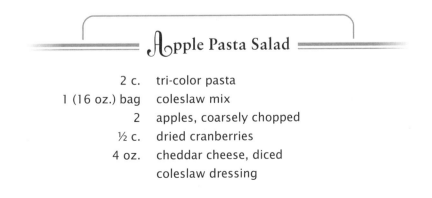

Apple Pasta Salad

2 c.	tri-color pasta
1 (16 oz.) bag	coleslaw mix
2	apples, coarsely chopped
½ c.	dried cranberries
4 oz.	cheddar cheese, diced
	coleslaw dressing

Cook pasta according to package directions. Drain and cool. Mix pasta with coleslaw mix, apples, cranberries, and cheddar cheese. Add dressing to your taste. Chill and serve.

Harvest Pork and Apples

1½–2 lbs.	pork loin
1–2 Tbs.	vegetable oil
	salt and pepper to taste
1 c.	apple cider or juice
2 lg.	Granny Smith apples, peeled and sliced
2 c.	butternut squash, peeled, seeded, and cubed
½ c.	brown sugar
¼ tsp.	cinnamon
¼ tsp.	dried thyme
¼ tsp.	dried sage

Heat oil in a skillet and brown pork loin on all sides, sprinkling with salt and pepper. Once browned, place in a greased slow cooker. Add apple cider. Mix remaining ingredients and place around pork loin. Cover and cook on low 5–6 hours or until pork is tender.

See You at the Pole

See You at the Pole occurs the fourth Wednesday in September. Started in 1990, this event is one in which students all over the nation and world gather to pray for their school and country. This event is often organized by pastors and youth workers, so be sure to check your local papers, community bulletin boards, or church youth group calendar for the times and schools participating.

Homeschool students also take part in See You at the Pole as they often gather at the local courthouse flagpole. This is a great day to use to talk to your kids about the importance of prayer and freedom of religion. You can even make it an annual fun tradition by including breakfast out at a local restaurant before you head to the pole.

Native American Day

Native American Day, the fourth Friday in September, was first established in California in 1968 by Ronald Reagan. This isn't a national holiday, but various states have adopted a similar day to honor some of the first residents in their area. Every continental state has a history of Native American tribes. Don't wait for your state to adopt a day in their honor to recognize their contributions both then and now to our country.

To learn more, research your own state's history. Visit museums, libraries, and cultural centers. Research recipes, art, dance, and music. There is a richness to our shared history we can appreciate and teach our children to appreciate.

Halloween

No other day on the calendar causes such passionate responses as Halloween. We find sincere Jesus-following people on all sides of the issue of how to handle this day. But rather than taking a side, we think of Halloween as a day when people need to hear about the love of Jesus—just like any other day on the calendar . . . maybe more so.

What other day will so many children come to your home? How can you take advantage of this opportunity to show God's love? What simple ways can you show kindness? How can you and your family be a light in a dark world? Here are some suggestions for honoring God with your life and home.

Pray silently for each child and family who come to your door.

Sit outside and offer hot chocolate to cold parents.

If you choose to give out candy, let each child know that God loves them.

Carve a pumpkin with your children and teach them the Pumpkin Prayer:

Dear God,
Open my mind so I can learn about You.
(Cut the top off the pumpkin.)
Take away all my sin and forgive me for the wrong things I do.
(Clean out the inside.)
Open my eyes so Your love I will see.
(Cut the eyes out in heart shapes.)
I'm so sorry for turning up my nose to all you've given me.
(Cut a nose in the shape of a cross.)
Open my ears so Your Word I will hear.
(Cut the ears rectangular-shaped like the Bible.)
Open my mouth so I can tell others You're near.
(Cut the mouth in the shape of a fish.)
Let Your light shine in all I say and do! Amen.
(Place a candle inside and light it.)

Shine your faith. Carve a pumpkin with the name of Jesus, and when people ask about it explain that Jesus is the Light of the world.

Harvest Celebrations

Finally, brothers and sisters, whatever is true, whatever is noble, whatever is right, whatever is pure, whatever is lovely, whatever is admirable—if anything is excellent or praiseworthy—think about such things.

Philippians 4:8

October is a beautiful time, especially in climates where God shows off by displaying vibrant, gorgeous colors in the changing leaves of the trees. Crops are harvested, apples are pressed into cider, and pumpkins are carved into smiling faces. All around are sensational smells and visual brightness. Autumn is also a perfect time to celebrate God's bounty and goodness to us and make some seasonal memories with our loved ones. So grab some cider and a donut (or two!) and get ready to fall into some fun!

SWING YOUR PARTNER

Fall is a perfect time to put out a call—to friends and family—and bring in a caller of the square-dancing sort. Host an old-fashioned square dance to joyfully celebrate God's abundant harvest. Have everyone bring a finger food to pass or a gallon of apple cider. You provide the plates and cups. Have yourselves a happy hoe-down!

> **Let us not become weary in doing good, for at the proper time we will reap a harvest if we do not give up.**
>
> ~ *Galatians 6:9*

RAISE THE FLAGS

Host a flag football party for kids or even adults. For a hearty but easy meal after the big game, throw a baked potato bar. You provide the baked potatoes (easily made in your slow cooker: wrap each potato in foil and bake on low for 8–10 hours; test for doneness by pricking with a fork, and then turn the slow cooker to the "keep warm" setting), and your guests provide the toppings, such as sour cream, butter, cheddar cheese, chopped cooked broccoli, ham, salsa, taco meat, pulled pork barbeque, and so forth. For dessert, serve donuts and hot cocoa. Here is a fabulous homemade recipe:

Homemade Hot Cocoa for a Crowd

Forget the powdered stuff! This rich and creamy confection is a delicious fall warmer-upper.

In a large kettle, combine:

2 c.	sugar
1⅓ c.	water
1 c.	cocoa powder
½ tsp.	salt

Heat over medium heat until mixture boils. Boil 1 minute, stirring constantly. Add 1 gallon whole milk and heat thoroughly, but do not boil. Remove from heat. Stir in 1 tablespoon vanilla or 2 teaspoons almond extract. Top with marshmallows or whipped cream as desired. Serve immediately. Makes about 16 8 oz. servings.

TAKE A HIKE

Find a park or nature center and take a fall hike. If you live in an area where the colors change, also take along a bag for collecting leaves. Be sure to pack a snack and a thermos of something hot to enjoy along the route. When home, press your leaves between wax paper with an iron set on low. Cut out and display on your window just like you did when you were little. A stroll in nature and a walk down memory lane—both at once!

RECIPES FOR HARVEST TIME

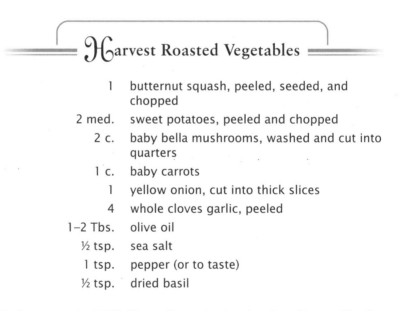

Harvest Roasted Vegetables

1	butternut squash, peeled, seeded, and chopped
2 med.	sweet potatoes, peeled and chopped
2 c.	baby bella mushrooms, washed and cut into quarters
1 c.	baby carrots
1	yellow onion, cut into thick slices
4	whole cloves garlic, peeled
1–2 Tbs.	olive oil
½ tsp.	sea salt
1 tsp.	pepper (or to taste)
½ tsp.	dried basil

Preheat oven to 450°F. Place all veggies in a bowl and toss with olive oil so they are well covered. Stir in salt, pepper, and basil. Place in a single layer on a baking sheet and bake for 40 minutes, turning halfway. Check at 30 minutes to see if mushrooms or onions are getting overdone. If so, remove and continue cooking remaining vegetables.

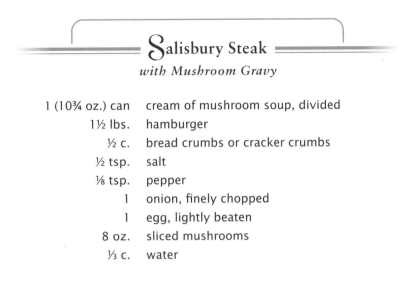

Salisbury Steak
with Mushroom Gravy

1 (10¾ oz.) can	cream of mushroom soup, divided
1½ lbs.	hamburger
½ c.	bread crumbs or cracker crumbs
½ tsp.	salt
⅛ tsp.	pepper
1	onion, finely chopped
1	egg, lightly beaten
8 oz.	sliced mushrooms
⅓ c.	water

Combine hamburger with ¼ can of soup, bread crumbs, salt, pepper, onion, and egg. Form into 6 patties. Fry each patty in a Dutch oven in a small amount of oil, removing from pan when browned. Combine remaining soup, water, and sliced mushrooms. Place three of the hamburger patties back into the Dutch oven and cover with half the soup mixture. Repeat with the other three patties and remaining soup mixture. Cover pan and cook over low heat for approximately 20 minutes, or until hamburger patties are cooked through. Serve with rice, if desired.

Peanut Butter Apple Crisp

Spray a 9 x 13 pan with cooking spray. Peel and slice enough Granny Smith or other tart cooking apples to fill the pan. Sprinkle apples with:

2 Tbs.	lemon juice
½ tsp.	salt

Mix together:

¼ c.	flour
¾ c.	sugar

Shake over the top of apples. Toss gently.

Combine topping ingredients:

½ c.	butter, softened
1 c.	chunky peanut butter

Add in:

½ tsp.	salt
1 c.	sugar
¾ c.	flour
1½ c.	old-fashioned rolled oats

Topping should hold together in clumps when pressed in your fist and not be too sticky. If it is, add a little more flour.

Sprinkle topping over apples and bake at 375°F for about 25–30 minutes, until apples are tender and topping is lightly golden. Serve with vanilla ice cream or whipped cream.

· · · · · · · · · · · · · Election Day · · · · · · · · · · · ·

Our election day in America is held on the Tuesday after the first Monday in November. (Those of you quick with math will realize this means the earliest it can be is November 2 and the latest is November 8.) Federal elections are held only on even years, and presidential elections are held every four years in years that are divisible by four.

Okay—enough about the numbers. Let's eat! For an election day breakfast, have some cherry-almond granola. (George Washington would be proud!) And to enjoy for dinner before you start watching the returns come in, try this famous soup recipe served daily in the United States Senate. It's delicious with some bread fresh out of the oven.

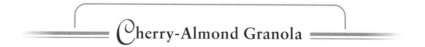

Cherry-Almond Granola

This dish pulls double duty. Not only is it a breakfast treat, but you can sprinkle it over vanilla ice cream and then drizzle it with honey for a clever, out-of-the-ordinary dessert!

4 c.	old-fashioned oats
1½ c.	sliced almonds
½ c.	light brown sugar, packed
½ tsp.	salt
½ tsp.	ground cinnamon
¼ tsp.	ground nutmeg
¼ c.	vegetable oil
¼ c.	honey
1 tsp.	almond extract
1½ c.	dried cherries

In a bowl, mix oats, almonds, brown sugar, salt, cinnamon, and nutmeg. In a saucepan, heat oil and honey over very low heat until blended well. Stir in almond extract. Pour over the oat mixture and mix well. Spread granola on a large cookie sheet that has been sprayed with cooking spray. Bake 35–40 minutes, stirring carefully every 10 minutes, until lightly golden. Place pan on a rack to cool. Stir in dried cherries. Cool completely. Seal granola in an airtight container. Store at room temperature for 1 week or in the freezer for 2 months.

Senate Navy Bean Soup

2 lbs.	dried navy beans
1 gal.	hot water
1½ lbs.	smoked ham hocks
1	onion, chopped
2 Tbs.	butter
	salt and pepper to taste

Wash the navy beans in a colander and run hot water over them until they are slightly whitened. Place beans into pot with 1 gallon hot water. Add ham hocks and simmer approximately 3 hours in a covered pot, stirring occasionally. Remove ham hocks and set aside to cool. Dice meat and return to soup. Lightly brown the onion in butter. Add to soup. Before serving, bring soup to a boil and season with salt and pepper. Serves 8.[2]

Note: If ham hocks frighten you, you can substitute 4 c. cooked, diced ham instead.

Veterans Day

November 11, Veterans Day, is observed on the closest Monday.

November 11 was originally Armistice Day and honored the ending of World War I. In 1954, President Eisenhower signed a bill proclaiming November 11 as Veterans Day. Veterans Day was set aside to honor all American veterans, both living and dead. In fact, Veterans Day is largely intended to thank *living* veterans for their dedicated and loyal service to their country.

The freedoms we have today are due to God's provision and to the sacrifices of men and women who have willingly risked their lives so that we can live safely. On November 11, take some time to let a veteran know how much you appreciate the sacrifice they made. But don't stop there. Pray about how you can support those actively serving today—and their families who make sacrifices as well. Here are a few ideas to get you started:

Make this a year-round effort. Research organizations that support veterans, those on active duty, reservists, and their families. Military. com has a comprehensive list. You might also try Wounded Warrior Project and Operation Gratitude.

Attend a Veterans Day service. Contact your local veterans' home to see if they are hosting any celebrations.

Reach out. Reach out to a veteran or someone currently in the service. Invite them to your home for a meal to say thank you.

Pause for prayer. At exactly 11 a.m. EST on November 11, a color guard made up of members from each of the military branches leads a ceremony at the Tomb of the Unknown Soldier in Arlington National

2. For more information about the history of this recipe, visit http://www.senate.gov/reference /reference_item/bean_soup.htm.

Cemetery to honor all those who have served in the service of our country. At this time, take a moment to pray for veterans and for all those currently serving.

Bless the family. Is there a military wife to whom you can bring a thank-you basket? Tuck in some special hand lotion, a scented candle, candy, and nail polish. Write a note acknowledging her part in the sacrifice. And don't forget the military husband left to manage a home and family while his wife serves. Bring a care basket with dinner, a movie, popcorn, and candy for the kids.

12

Celebrate the Sights and Scents of the Seasons

The heat of summer wanes, a snap is in the morning air, and autumn colors on trees and in store windows announce the change of seasons. Celebrate this change in small ways. Here are some suggestions:

Pumpkin vases. Hollow out pumpkins of various sizes and use them as planters for fall flowers such as mums, asters, and sunflowers.

Create leaf rubbings. This is a great family activity that produces pretty fall artwork. You'll need a variety of leaves, thin paper, and crayons or oil pastels. Place paper over leaf and rub gently with a crayon. Rub only to the edge of the leaf. You can overlap the leaves on a single sheet of paper to create a collage. Or cut out the leaves and make a leaf banner.

Celebrate the scents. Candles are always good, but you can also make your own potpourri by simmering orange slices, whole cloves, and cinnamon sticks in a small amount of water.

Make dried fruit ornaments. All you need is fruit (apples, oranges, pears, lemons), clear varnish, and twine. To make, slice fruit thinly, saving the ends for potpourri. Dry fruit in 175°F oven for about 7 hours, turning occasionally. Once dry and cooled, cover both sides with clear craft varnish. Punch a hole in each slice and thread through a 6-inch piece of twine. Use as decorations around your home.

Make your own coffee syrup. Do you love pumpkin spice lattes, but not the price? Try making your own coffee syrup. Here's a recipe for pumpkin spice:

Pumpkin Spice Syrup

1½ c.	water
1½ c.	sugar
1 tsp.	ground nutmeg
½ tsp.	ground ginger
½ tsp.	ground cloves
3 Tbs.	pumpkin purée
4 (2–3 inch)	cinnamon sticks

Make sugar syrup by placing water and sugar in a saucepan over medium heat. Heat, stirring, until dissolved. Whisk in nutmeg, ginger, cloves, and pumpkin. Add cinnamon sticks and continue simmering for another 5–10 minutes. Allow to cool. Strain mixture through cheesecloth and store in sealed container in refrigerator for up to 3 weeks.

To make your own latte, combine 1 shot of espresso (instant is good, or use 2 oz. strong coffee) with 6 oz. warmed milk. Add syrup to taste.

· · · · · · · · · · · Thanksgiving · · · · · · · · · · ·

There, in the presence of the Lord your God, you and your families shall eat and shall rejoice in everything you have put your hand to, because the Lord your God has blessed you.

Deuteronomy 12:7

Since 1789, when President George Washington declared that there be a celebration of feasting and thanksgiving, Americans have been celebrating around the table with loved ones on the fourth Thursday of November.

Turkey may be at the center of our tables, but thankfulness should be in the center of our hearts and our thoughts. Let's keep the focus of Thanksgiving on thankfulness.

It's so easy to become discontent these days. Whether through television, Facebook, or music, we see other people flaunt what they have . . . and consequently, what we have doesn't seem so nice any more.

We are content with our three-bedroom house—until we see a four-bedroom house on HGTV.

Our MP3 player was enough—until we compared it with someone's new iPod.

Checking books out of the library was great—until we see someone's Kindle that can hold hundreds of books.

Comparisons destroy thankfulness.

The best way we've found to be content with what we have is to focus on being thankful. Here are a few practical ways to make Thanksgiving about more than food and football.

Create a countdown calendar. Create your own "Countdown to Thanksgiving" calendar by cutting shapes of leaves in different colors. Make one for every day from November 1 until Thanksgiving. Number them and tape them onto the refrigerator. Every day, write one thing you are thankful to God for on the leaf for that day. By Thanksgiving your refrigerator will be filled with reminders of all God has given your family.

Keep a thankfulness journal as a family. Every day, fill in something you are thankful for and why. For example, I'm thankful for my fingers so I can write. Or, my husband is thankful that we live where winters are warm so he can run. Start it on Thanksgiving Day and take turns writing in your journal as often as you can throughout the year. Make sure you date it so you can look back and remember.

Welcome singles. Do you know someone who might be alone on Thanksgiving? Invite them to join your family for dinner. Offer to pick them up if driving is a challenge.

Plan an outreach project. After dinner is over on Thanksgiving, discuss as a family how you will reach out to others in the coming Christmas season. Be intentional in scheduling time to do this in the coming weeks as a family.

Host a theme dinner. Try your hand at a colonial Thanksgiving dinner, or another theme that suits your family—perhaps one that reminds you of a recent vacation or other favorite place.

Glynnis

It started the year our immediate family went to Colonial Williamsburg, where I purchased a cookbook. The experience charmed and delighted me. So when Thanksgiving rolled around a few months later, I decided to see if I could recreate that experience for my extended family, at least from a food perspective.

> **They celebrate your abundant goodness and joyfully sing of your righteousness.**
>
> ~ *Psalm 145:7*

It's not that I don't love tradition, but I really like trying new things. Combine that experimental mentality with a love for history and travel, and an idea was born. I would try a colonial Thanksgiving dinner.

I pitched the idea to my mother, sisters, and niece, since we are the team that was assembling dinner, and they loved it. Next, it was time to create the menu.

Since I had purchased a cookbook on our trip, I started there. The menu included leek and potato soup, corn pudding, Sally Lunn rolls, and oyster stuffing. Since turkey was enjoyed in colonial times, we had that as well. I copied recipes and made assignments.

The idea was so successful we continued it for years. Our themes have included Hawaiian (including Haupia pie for dessert), South Carolina Low Country, Mexican, and New Orleans.

RECIPES FOR THANKSGIVING

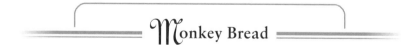

Monkey Bread

Make this family favorite for an easy breakfast while you are getting a jump-start on the big meal.

3 cans	biscuits, cut into 4 pieces each (buy the larger biscuits)
1 Tbs.	cinnamon

1 c.   granulated sugar
½ c.   butter or margarine, melted
1 c.   brown sugar

Preheat oven to 350°F. Grease Bundt pan. Put cinnamon, sugar, and cut biscuit pieces in a small paper bag and shake well to coat. Place biscuit pieces in Bundt pan. Mix melted butter and brown sugar and pour over biscuits. Bake at 350°F for 30 minutes or until golden brown. Invert on a serving platter to serve. Serve with breakfast meat or fresh fruit and juice.

Oven Roasted Sweet Potatoes and Apples

A unique side dish that goes perfectly with turkey!

3 lg.   sweet potatoes, peeled and sliced thin
3   Granny Smith apples, peeled and sliced
½ c.   brown sugar
1 tsp. cinnamon
¼ c.   apple juice
2 Tbs. butter

Overlap sweet potato and apple slices in a 9 x 13 baking dish, alternating between apple and sweet potato. Mix brown sugar and cinnamon in apple juice and pour over apples and potato. Dot with butter. Cover with foil and bake in a 400°F oven for 35–45 minutes or until easily pierced with a fork. Remove foil for last 5 minutes to caramelize the top.

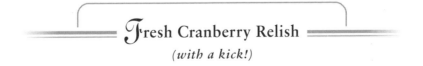

Fresh Cranberry Relish
(with a kick!)

This is unlike any traditional cranberry relish we've tried. Crunchy with a slight kick. Make it the day before for best flavor.

4 c.   chopped fresh cranberries
¼ tsp. ground ginger
2   jalapeños, finely chopped

½	red onion, minced
4	seedless oranges, peeled and finely chopped
3 stalks	celery, minced
1 c.	sugar

Mix all and cover. Store in the refrigerator. Use within one week.

Creamy Gratin of Winter Root Vegetables

Who knew veggies could taste so gourmet?

3 lg.	parsnips
2 sm.	rutabagas
1 med.	turnip
3	Yukon gold potatoes
1 Tbs.	coarse sea salt or kosher salt
2 tsp.	fine sea salt
1 tsp.	pepper
½ c.	half-and-half
½ c.	whole milk
2 Tbs. + 1 tsp.	unsalted butter, divided
4 Tbs.	fresh parsley, minced, divided
3 Tbs.	Parmesan cheese, grated
3 Tbs.	Gruyere cheese

Preheat oven to 350°F. Butter a 9 x 13 baking dish. Peel the root vegetables and cut into 1-inch cubes. Place in a stockpot and cover with water, adding coarse salt. Bring to a boil, then reduce to medium and cook uncovered approximately 30 minutes, or until a fork easily pierces the vegetables. Drain vegetables and transfer to a large bowl. Sprinkle with sea salt and pepper. Meanwhile heat half-and-half, milk, and 2 tablespoons butter. Mash vegetables with the cream mixture and 3 tablespoons parsley. Spoon into prepared baking dish. Top with cheeses and dot with remaining teaspoon of butter. Bake 20 minutes, until golden. To get a crispy top, heat the broiler and

> **Give thanks to the LORD, for he is good; his love endures forever.**
>
> ~ *Psalm 107:1*

place the pan under it for about 5 minutes. Sprinkle with remaining parsley to serve.

Pumpkin Crème Brulee

Pumpkin pie's fancy cousin. Your guests will adore this once-a-year decadent treat!

2 c.	pumpkin purée
½ c.	sugar
¼ c.	margarine or butter, melted
½ tsp.	cinnamon
2	eggs

• Custard

2 c.	whipping cream or heavy cream
½ c.	white sugar
4 lg.	egg yolks
1 tsp.	vanilla extract

• Topping

⅓ c.	brown sugar

Combine pumpkin, sugar, melted butter, cinnamon, and eggs. Use electric mixer to blend until smooth. Spread into bottom of an 8 x 8 baking dish.

Place the custard ingredients into saucepan and whisk lightly to combine. Heat over medium low, whisking constantly, for 5 minutes or until just warm. Pour custard over pumpkin.

Place baking dish in the center of larger baking dish, and pour water into larger dish until it is about an inch deep.

Bake at 325°F for 1 hour or until knife inserted in center comes out almost clean. Cool on a wire rack. Once cool, cover and refrigerate for several hours or overnight. Before serving, allow to sit at room temperature for half an hour. Sprinkle brown sugar over top and place under the broiler for 5 minutes or so. Don't walk away! Remove when sugar is caramelized nicely.

Christmas

> And he will be called
> Wonderful Counselor, Mighty God,
> Everlasting Father, Prince of Peace.
> Isaiah 9:6

"Sleigh bells ring . . . Are you stressin'?" No time of year brings more happiness and delight—while at the same time tension and headaches—than Christmas. While we long for a memorable holiday with fresh homemade goodies, stunning décor, and gifts that are *just* right, our best intentions don't always come to fruition.

We stress about the finances, fret about the food, and get hassled by the holiday décor. In the end, we don't always discover the delight, the simplicity, or the true gift of Christmas. Instead, we collapse on the couch in exhaustion, vowing next year will be different.

It doesn't have to be this way. By planning ahead, setting realistic expectations, and determining what works best for *your* family, you can have the Christmas you've always wanted. A Christmas filled only with the activities and traditions that matter most. A Christmas centered around family and loved ones, filled with memorable moments that will last a lifetime.

Wise Women Still Seek Him

> You will seek me and find me when you seek me with all your heart.
> Jeremiah 29:13

In the midst of shopping, tinseling, frosting, and wrapping, we can easily miss the true meaning of Christmas. Too many activities combined with the stress of trying to do it all leave us feeling exhausted and empty.

This festive frenzy is really nothing new. Even in the account found in the Gospel of Luke during that first Christmas in Bethlehem, urgency was afoot. A quick read through chapter 2 finds an angel *abruptly* appearing, a heavenly host *suddenly* filling the sky, simple shepherds deciding *at once* to go examine the scene for themselves, and the words "*so they hurried off*" chosen to describe that investigative journey.

However, in the center of that fast-paced story we find two simple words: "But Mary."

> But Mary was keeping within herself all these things (sayings), weighing and pondering them in her heart.
>
> Luke 2:19 AMP

When the mother of the baby King is mentioned, the hustle halts. She isn't depicted as scurrying and hurrying. No. She is weighing and pondering. Her contemplating goes beyond the commotion, right to the heart of what the hustle is all about.

Jesus.

Jesus, the Savior of the world. The calm in our chaos.

Weighing and pondering.

Could *we* do the same? Could we dare find calm in the Christmas chaos? A holy hush among the hustle? More importantly, could we model for the wide-eyed kids in our lives just how to slow down and, like the wise men of old, actually *look* for the Savior?

PREPARING ROOM IN OUR HEARTS FOR HIM

Advent is a season of anticipation. We make our hearts ready for the celebration of the birth of Jesus. Intentionally celebrating Advent can help us keep our eyes and activities focused on Christ and off of the secular trappings of the season (although those are fun and fine!).

Advent begins the fourth Sunday before December 25, so plans to celebrate need to be made in November. Try some of these ideas on for size.

AN ADVENT ADVENTURE

For decades Christians have used an Advent wreath to usher in the celebration of Christ's birth. Traditionally there are three purple candles and one pink one, along with a white candle for the center, in an Advent wreath. Whether you purchase a traditional Advent wreath or make your own unique adaptation (four blue mason jars and one clear jar holding tea lights nestled in an antique basket and accented with spruce branches, or five votive candle holders on a mirror in the middle of the kitchen table, or . . . anything goes), an Advent candle tradition is a sure-fire way (pun intended) to bring hope and anticipation to Christmas.

> *On the first Sunday of Advent*, we have the first purple candle, known as the "candle of hope," representing the prophecy of the birth of Christ. Read Isaiah 7:14, Romans 15:12–13, and 1 John 4:9 as you light the flame.

> *On the second Sunday*, light the first purple candle and the second purple candle. This second candle is the "candle of preparation," which represents Bethlehem. Read Luke 1:26–28 and Luke 2:1–7.

> *On the third Sunday of Advent*, light the first two purple candles and the pink candle, which is known as the "candle of joy." This one represents the angels who announced Christ's birth. Read Luke 2:8–16.

> *On the fourth Sunday*, light the first two purple candles, the pink candle, and the third purple candle, the "candle of love," which is a representation of God's love. Read John 3:16–17 and 1 John 4:9–11.

> *On Christmas Eve*, light all of the candles, including the white "Christ candle" in the center. These are a flickering reminder that Christmas is about Jesus, the Light of the World! Read John 8:12 and discuss ways you can be His light to those you come in contact with.

Seeking Baby Jesus

Each year, as our Christmas decorations are unpacked, I take the manger and/or Baby Jesus out of all the nativity scenes in the house before they are set up. The nativity stays that way, with Mary, Joseph, shepherds, wise men, and animals only until Christmas Eve. Then, when everyone else is asleep, I tuck Baby Jesus into the manger scenes! The girls were always excited on Christmas morning to check to see "if Jesus came." Now that they are older, if they get to the decorating before me, they still take out the Jesus figurines and give them to me for safekeeping until Christmas! It's a fun way to keep Christ in CHRISTmas and always gave the girls something to look for on Christmas morning that we felt was even more important than the goodies that their stockings held.

Sheila

SIMPLIFY YOUR CELEBRATION

Got holiday stress?

We know you do. Here is a great way to re-evaluate your holidays and make them less about the hustle and more about Him.

Gather everyone around the kitchen table to answer questions about your family celebration. Encourage everyone to be honest with their responses and promise no hurt feelings. The goal is to discover your unique way of celebrating the holidays and help alleviate some of the Yuletide "Yikes!" Here are some questions to get you started:

What has been your favorite family tradition over the years and why?

What has been your least favorite holiday tradition and why?

Have the adults share their favorite memory of their holidays growing up. Did it have to do more with money or with people, with getting or with doing?

Can you think of any new tradition you would like to start celebrating and why?

What holiday foods do you really love and most look forward to?

What holiday foods could you do without?

How can we divide up tasks during the holidays?

Don't take it personally if your family tells you they don't like your great aunt's fruitcake or some other treat you faithfully make each year. This just means you won't have to make it this year! Your goal is to lighten your load and simplify your holidays.

Once you have reevaluated your December calendar and eliminated activities and events that aren't meaningful for your family, take a closer look at what remains. By keeping Christ at the core of your activities and traditions, you will provide a spiritually meaningful Christmas for yourself, your family, and everyone God brings into your home. And you will create a lifetime of wonderful memories for those you hold dear.

His Calm in the Chaos

> But the angel said to them, "Do not be afraid. I bring you good news that will cause great joy for all the people . . . a Savior has been born to you; he is the Messiah, the Lord."
>
> Luke 2:10–11

Don't let your own alone time with God suffer due to the increased demands in December. When our hearts are empty and our spiritual tank runs dry, we are less likely to experience His peace, His presence, and His hope as we celebrate His birthday. We need to intentionally draw away from the crowds to spend time with Jesus. Try these ideas to connect your heart with Christ before you attempt to celebrate with others.

Grab your Bible and a journal or notebook and something to write with. Sit near the lighted tree or light a fragrant Christmas candle. Start working your way through the Scriptures that tell the account of Christ's birth: Matthew 1–2 and Luke 1.

Don't just read. Absorb. Use a commentary to dig deeper. Or use the Amplified Version of the Bible, which expounds upon the meaning of the words in parentheses. Write down each day what you observe. Then ask yourself how it applies to you. Is there something you can learn? Something you need to change? Be intentional this year to really let the words of the nativity sink deep into your soul rather than just reading them like a fictional storybook.

Purchase a Christmas-themed devotional book such as *God Is in the Manger: Reflections on Advent and Christmas* by Dietrich Bonhoeffer or *Once-A-Day 25 Days of Advent Devotional* published by Zondervan. Make a daily date with God as you work your way through the book.

Craft your own Christmas gift list. Pray about what you can "give to Jesus" as a gift this season. Is it time with Him? Prayer? Kindness to strangers? A Bible verse you will memorize each week? A charitable contribution to a mission or missionary? Service at a homeless shelter? What can you give Christ as an offering of gratitude for what He did for you by becoming flesh and coming to earth?

For another list-making idea, ponder the many Christmases past. What fond memories do you have? What gifts do you recall receiving that were particularly meaningful? Write them down. Thank God for the experiences and people that have shaped your holidays.

What if the holidays hold painful memories for you? Write them down too. Then ask Jesus to help shape your perspective, to turn those scarred places and painful ponderings into good. If you grew up in a home with domestic violence, perhaps you could visit a shelter and serve a meal or babysit children while the mothers hold a Bible study. If you grew up in a single-parent home, offer to take a child who is in a similar situation Christmas shopping for their mother or father.

IT'S ALL ABOUT THE BABY

While there is certainly lots of fun to be had and memories to be made with some of the secular aspects of Christmas, here are some activities that can help you and your kiddos focus on Jesus at this time of year.

Attend a live nativity. Yes, live as in with real animals! Check the internet or your local paper for churches that hold one. Since the animals don't always get their acting cues right, you might be in for a real show!

Tell the Christmas story in cookies. Turn an ordinary Saturday afternoon into the sweetest story ever told. Invite your children and a few friends over to make sugar cookies with very specific shapes: angel, star, tree, heart, and bell. As they decorate, tell about the miracle of Christmas:

An *angel* told Mary she would carry the Savior and told the shepherds about His birth.

The wise men followed the *star* to get to Jesus.

They brought precious gifts like the kind we have under our *tree*.

The best gift of all that day was Jesus. God sent His only Son so that whoever accepts Jesus into their *heart* will live forever with God in heaven.

The *bell* rings for joy as we celebrate Jesus's birthday and God's gift to us.

Host a birthday party for Jesus. Send out invitations, asking everyone to bring an unwrapped toy that will be donated. Have party games with a slight twist (for example, play Angel rather than Bingo). Bake a cake, have streamers, and really celebrate the birth of Jesus.

SHOP, BUT DON'T DROP!

Each of you should give what you have decided in your heart to give, not reluctantly or under compulsion, for God loves a cheerful giver.

2 Corinthians 9:7

While Christmas may still mean family, lights, and making cutout cookies, what is often on the minds of kids and adults alike is, *What is in it for me?* Contrast that with Jesus, who said, "It is more blessed to give than to receive" (Acts 20:35).

If we want to stay true to the words of Jesus and also recapture the simplicity of Christmases past—where *people* and *giving* were more treasured than *objects* and *getting*—we need to be intentional with our gift-giving.

Let's see exchanging gifts as a challenge, not a burden. And as a way to reach out and model the true meaning of Christmas to those who will untie the pretty ribbons on our gifts.

REACHING IN AND REACHING OUT

It is Christmas every time you let God love others through you.

Mother Teresa

At this time of year, even though family comes first, fight the temptation to make your holidays "family only." Christmas is often a lonely time for those facing a job loss or foreclosure, the death of a family member, or the breakup of a marriage. Some have an empty spot at the holiday table that is usually occupied by someone now serving in another country. Others have had sons or daughters move far away or a family feud that has left them celebrating alone.

Christmas is an excuse to make someone else's life better. The memories of the very best kind are the ones where we are not so wrapped up in ourselves. Giving instead of receiving is what fills us the most and creates the sweetest memories.

Purpose this year to reach out during this season. Ask the Lord to show you who might be encouraged with a little love. As you dish it out, it is sure to spill all over you too! Here are some concepts to get you started:

Go on a mission. Together as a family, visit a nursing home, deliver dry goods to food pantries, or serve meals at your local homeless or battered women's shelter or soup kitchen. Spread the love of Jesus by serving "the least of these" in His name. (And remember, people are hungry all year, not just at Christmas.)

See if your pastor will deliver a gift anonymously for you. Pack up some groceries or purchase a gas or department store gift card and see if it can be presented to a family in need of help during the holidays. You can do this as a family or with a group of friends, coworkers, or a small group.

Help an elderly person who is all alone during the season. Bring Christmas music and let it play as you and your kids help decorate their Christmas tree. Assist them with their holiday shopping and wrapping. Invite them to join your family for Christmas dinner. Take them to watch your kids in the church Christmas pageant. (They love seeing the kids recite their verses and sing their songs!) The holidays are often lonely, and these simple gestures will perk them up and provide much-needed companionship.

Adopt a military service member serving overseas or help the family of a deployed soldier. You can put together a care package for the soldier far away. Be sure to include a phone card so they can call home.

Put together treat baskets or platters for your local fire department, police department, teachers, church staff, healthcare workers, and so forth. Anyone who serves in the community would be encouraged to know they are appreciated. If this might raise safety concerns, have it delivered from a well-known local store. Include a note from Jesus and send it anonymously! (*Note*: not all places can accept homemade goodies. Please check with a supervisor before leaving anything that isn't store-bought.)

Secretly leave gifts or gift cards for families you know could use a little help. Do this totally under the radar. Your family will have so much fun being Jesus and keeping the secret!

Take a child whose parents have recently divorced to buy a gift for their mom or dad if you think the ex-spouse will not do so.

Invite a child or teen you know who will not have much of a holiday this year over for dinner. Allow them to join in with your family activities and feel the love of Christ in your home.

Make snowmen outside the room windows of nursing home patients or kids in the children's wing of a hospital. Don't forget the carrot nose and corncob pipe!

Scrape random windshields at the grocery store on a snowy and busy shopping day. Leave a laminated notecard that reads, "Random act of kindness. Pass it on."

Organize a "Twelve Days of Christmas" for a family in transition. When a dear family friend of Karen's was facing his first Christmas as a divorced father of five, she knew his transition would be rough. Raising his kids in a new home without the entire family together was a recipe for sadness. To add some cheer and anticipation, she gathered twelve families, who each left a gift on the father's porch for as many days in a row. There were baskets of food, bright buckets of snacks with movie passes, gift cards, and presents for the kids, certificates for restaurants, and certificates for buying all-new Christmas decorations and a tree. Each one had a handwritten card with well-wishes or a prayer for the family. This Twelve Days of Christmas was a way to add a bright spot to this hurting family's holiday season, and the father relayed to Karen how his kids were so excited each day to wake up and see what had been left for them!

THE RICHNESS OF TRADITIONS

Traditions run deep and last long. While some traditions are passed down from generation to generation, others are born out of the desire to create meaningful memories for your family. These activities and special foods

· · · · · · · · · · **Lynn Cowell** · · · · · · · · ·

Proverbs 31 Ministries

When I first started mentoring teen girls, I was completely shocked that many of them just never got involved in the kitchen! There was a variety of reasons: "My mom doesn't like me to get the kitchen messy," "She likes to do it her way on her own," or "My mom doesn't cook." Whatever the reason, nothing draws out great conversations like cooking or baking together. Each year, I invite the girls I hang out with to make my kitchen a mess! At Christmas, we always create at least three or four goodies we share with the elderly in our lives (and eat plenty for ourselves as we go!). Having a theme night is also a lot of fun: Mexican, Italian . . . anything that allows them to get a little experience with an oven and a recipe!

The night of our get-together, I start with several recipes and all of the ingredients set up at "stations" in my kitchen. Putting the girls in pairs, I let them get after it. Watching them learn how to read a recipe is half the fun! Sometimes it turns out, and other times it is a complete disaster. One thing that is a guarantee: I'm given a few moments to chat about life stuff, share Jesus, and let them know they are incredibly loved!

bind families together and deposit memories in their hearts that will warm them for years to come.

It's not necessary to spend a lot of money or plan elaborate holiday celebrations to begin or continue a Christmas tradition. A tradition can be as simple as eating homemade caramel corn the night you decorate your Christmas tree.

Traditions can stem from your heritage. They can be a recipe. If it's not Christmas without Grandma Elsie's divinity fudge, then Grandma Elsie's divinity fudge is a tradition. If you watch *Christmas with the Kranks* each year snuggled up as a family, then that spells tradition to your kids for years to come. Two components comprise traditions: meaning and frequency.

If you experience, eat, watch, do, or perform something and it has meaning for your family, this is step one. If your family wants to repeat it the next year—a tradition is born.

If your season is full of activities that have meaning and your family wants to repeat, you already have tradition working in your favor. Perhaps you can focus on picking an item or two from the outreach section of this chapter to brighten the holiday.

On the other hand, if you desire to add a meaningful family Christmas tradition or two to your holiday celebration, here are some great ideas that will create memories and can be passed on from generation to generation.

YULETIDE SCAVENGER HUNT

Ten years ago, the year my hubby Dave died, I was simply overwhelmed with Christmas and all the "stuff" surrounding it. I had gifts for the girls but wanted to make opening their last gift—which was something their dad had talked about getting them, a small foosball table—special. I came up with the idea of a last-gift scavenger hunt.

Under the tree was a gift bag addressed to both girls. Inside was an invitation to the first annual Christmas scavenger hunt and clue #1. Clues led them all around the house, into the yard, onto the neighbor's front porch—I think there were fourteen in all that year!

They ended up in the garage where the foosball table sat with a big bow on it. We have continued that tradition for nearly ten years! Even the eighteen-year-old gets excited about the hunt. I have sent them to the park in our neighborhood, onto the roof, to ask a neighbor for a clue, and even into the attic. It all depends how tired mama is on Christmas Eve at midnight. I think it stretches out our Christmas morning and helps slow us down. I love seeing them work together!

Danita H.

CHRISTMAS CARD PROJECTS

Christmas cards can be used in many ways. Here are a few ideas.

Save all the cards, and then after Christmas pick one a day and pray for the giver of the card.

Cut them apart to make gift tags for the next year. Get creative by gluing the cutouts to colored paper or scrapbook paper and adorn with stickers and glitter pens.

Use them to make placecards for the Christmas table. Cut pieces of white cardstock. Fold in half. Glue cutout pictures onto the white card, allowing half of the cutout to rise above the fold. Write the name of the guest on the bottom.

BEYOND FRUITCAKE AND FUDGE

So many of our best memories of the holidays were made in the kitchen: the smell of sugar cookies cooling while we peered over the edge of the counter on tip-toe in our eagerness to frost them, the aroma of a turkey cooking, or the scent of mulled cider brewing. But all the holiday baking can certainly take its toll! So here are some practical tips to help make your holiday baking a little easier but just as yummy.

> **Blessed is the season which engages the whole world in a conspiracy of love.**
>
> ~ *Hamilton Wright Mabie*

Organize a goodies swap. Gather a group of friends and have each bring three dozen (or any number) of one kind of cookie, fudge, or candy, plus containers to take treats home. Place all the goodies on a counter and allow everyone to choose an assortment to take home equal to the number of goodies they brought. Turn on the Christmas music and swap goodies and stories. Everyone will end up with a variety of treats even though they only made one!

Share the load with a friend. Invite a friend over, share in the cost of ingredients, split the shopping, and do your baking together. This works great if you want to give food as gifts or simply have your freezer stocked.

HOLIDAY LOVIN' FROM YOUR OVEN

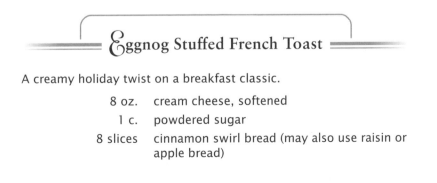

Eggnog Stuffed French Toast

A creamy holiday twist on a breakfast classic.

8 oz.	cream cheese, softened
1 c.	powdered sugar
8 slices	cinnamon swirl bread (may also use raisin or apple bread)

4	eggs, beaten
¾ c.	real eggnog
1 Tbs.	sugar
½ tsp.	nutmeg (fresh-grated is best)

Blend cream cheese and powdered sugar in a small bowl. Spread the mixture on 4 slices of bread and then top each with a second piece of bread to make 4 sandwiches. Mix all remaining ingredients in a shallow dish. Coat sandwiches in egg mixture on both sides and fry on a buttered griddle over medium heat (325°F on an electric griddle), turning once. Serve with real maple syrup and butter. (Come on—it's Christmas! Spring for the real stuff!)

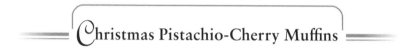

Christmas Pistachio-Cherry Muffins

These simple and delicious red and green muffins make a great teacher gift!

1 box	white cake mix
1 sm. box	instant pistachio pudding mix
1 (10 oz.) jar	maraschino cherries, drained, coarsely chopped, and tossed in 1 Tbs. flour
	white sugar
	Christmas cupcake liners

Mix cake batter according to box directions and add in dry pudding mix. (Do not make the actual pudding, just add the dry mix to the cake mix.) Gently stir in drained cherries. Spoon into muffin tins lined with papers. Sprinkle a little white sugar on top of each. Bake according to box directions for muffins, or just a bit less. Do not over bake.

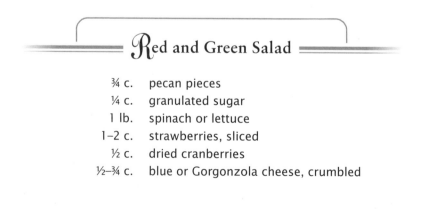

Red and Green Salad

¾ c.	pecan pieces
¼ c.	granulated sugar
1 lb.	spinach or lettuce
1–2 c.	strawberries, sliced
½ c.	dried cranberries
½–¾ c.	blue or Gorgonzola cheese, crumbled

• Dressing

¼ c.	apple cider vinegar
1 Tbs.	minced shallots
2 Tbs.	honey
1 Tbs.	Dijon mustard
2 c.	vegetable oil

To make sugared pecans, put granulated sugar in a small frying pan. Add pecan pieces. Turn burner to medium and stir constantly. The sugar will melt within a few minutes. Quickly stir the nuts to coat and remove immediately from heat or the nuts will burn. Pour onto a lightly greased cookie sheet to cool. Break apart.

Wash spinach well and remove stems. Tear into bite sized pieces. For dressing, combine all ingredients and mix thoroughly. To serve, prepare salads in individual bowls to retain the presentation and assure that everyone gets an equal amount of strawberries, cranberries, cheese, and sugared nuts. Serves 6–8.

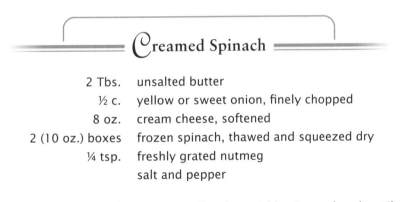

Creamed Spinach

2 Tbs.	unsalted butter
½ c.	yellow or sweet onion, finely chopped
8 oz.	cream cheese, softened
2 (10 oz.) boxes	frozen spinach, thawed and squeezed dry
¼ tsp.	freshly grated nutmeg
	salt and pepper

Melt butter in a sauté pan over medium heat. Add onion and cook until soft, about 8 minutes. Whisk in the cream cheese and let melt. Stir in the spinach until thoroughly combined and heated through. Add up to 3 tablespoons water if the mixture seems too dry. Add nutmeg and season with salt and pepper to taste.

An option for cheese lovers is to transfer spinach mixture to an oven-proof container, top with Parmesan or mozzarella cheese, and set under a broiler for a few minutes to melt. Serves 6–8.

Individual Beef Wellington

6 (8 oz.)	beef tenderloin steaks (1½–2 inches thick)
2 Tbs.	butter
3 sheets	frozen puff pastry, thawed
1	egg, lightly beaten

• *Mushroom Duxelles*

8 oz.	white button mushrooms, washed, trimmed, and roughly chopped
1	shallot, peeled and roughly chopped
1	clove garlic, quartered
2 tsp.	fresh thyme leaves
1 Tbs.	butter
1 Tbs.	olive oil
	salt and freshly ground black pepper

For mushroom duxelles, place mushrooms, shallot, garlic, and thyme in a food processor. Pulse until the mixture is very finely chopped, just short of becoming a paste. Heat butter and olive oil in pan over medium heat. Add mushroom mixture and cook until any liquid has evaporated and mushrooms are nicely browned. Season to taste with salt and freshly ground pepper as the mixture cooks. Set aside to cool.

For beef, brown steaks in butter for 2–3 minutes on each side. Remove and keep warm. Divide the mushroom mixture into 6 equal portions and spread across the top of each steak.

On a lightly floured surface, roll each puff pastry sheet into a 7 x 14 rectangle. Cut each into two 7-inch squares. Place a steak, mushroom side down, in the center of each square. Lightly brush pastry edges with water. Bring up opposite corners of pastry over steak; pinch seams to seal tightly. Cut 4 small slits in top of each pastry.

Place steaks in a greased baking pan. Brush with egg. Bake at 400°F for 25–30 minutes or until pastry is golden brown and meat reaches desired doneness (for medium-rare, a thermometer should read 145°F; medium, 160°F; well-done, 170°F).

Gingerbread Trifle

1 box	gingerbread mix
2 (4.6 oz.) boxes	cook-and-serve vanilla pudding
2 c.	whipping cream
2–4 Tbs.	sugar (to taste)
1 c.	English toffee chips
	ginger man cookies (such as Pepperidge Farm)

Prepare gingerbread mix according to package. Bake and allow to cool. Prepare vanilla pudding according to package directions and allow to cool. When ready to assemble, whip cream with electric mixer until soft peaks form. Add sugar and mix one more time. Serve in individual parfait glasses or pretty goblets for biggest impact. Layer cubed gingerbread, vanilla pudding, toffee bits, and whipped cream. Repeat and top with a cookie and an additional sprinkle of toffee bits. Makes 8–12 servings, depending on the size of goblets.

THREE KINGS AND THREE THINGS TRADITION

Karen

While my husband and I have made mistakes in rearing our brood, resulting in some "I wish we could go back and do *that* all over again" feelings, there is one decision we have never regretted. That is our decision as new parents to simplify Christmas gift-giving and NOT spoil and splurge and give in to our kids' every whim (and go into debt in the process).

Every year since our daughter Kenna was born (over twenty-two years ago), at Christmas our kids have received:

One thing to open on Christmas Eve (usually pjs, slippers, or a stuffed animal) that they can use right then as they try to fall asleep with all the excitement.

In the morning, a stocking full of treasures and treats.

And then, three gifts from us.

What? Did she say only three gifts?

Yep . . . I said three. That is all baby Jesus received from the kings—remember gold, frankincense, and myrrh? (And by way of trivia, do you

• • • • • • • • • **Karen** • • • • • • • •

Book 'Em!

One of my favorite gifts to give through the years has been book-based baskets. In my first book *Homespun Gifts from the Heart*, my coauthors (and dear friends), Trish and Kelly, and I devoted an entire chapter to book baskets and bundles. This is a unique gift-giving idea that encourages reading and is a snap to come up with.

Simply choose a book your recipient would love to read. *Then*, brainstorm on the topic (or leaf through the pages) to find items to round out the gift. Combine the items in a basket, add some clear cellophane, a ribbon and gift tag, and voila! You have a hit on your hands. Here are a few examples.

The first time I ever witnessed this idea was when my daughter received a Laura Ingalls Wilder basket. In it was an antique copy of *Little House in the Big Woods*. The rest of the surprise contained items Laura had gotten for Christmas in the late 1800s—a shiny new penny, a peppermint stick, a heart-shaped cookie sprinkled with white sugar, a tin cup, and a rag doll named Charlotte.

Know someone who is a culinary whiz? Try a cookbook with some measuring spoons and cups or a gadget such as a pastry blender or fancy chopper. Add jars of spices and seasonings and a fancy bottle of fruity spritzer for your loved one to sip on while cooking. Tuck a small wooden spoon into the bow.

What should you give to a baseball lover? Pick up a biography of a Major League legend such as Hank Aaron or Willie Mays, or even a current standout (my boys love Albert Pujols and Josh Hamilton). Round out the basket with some Big League Chew gum, a bag of sunflower seeds, a Baby Ruth candy bar, and tickets to a ball game. For filler, use peanuts in the shell, just like at the real ballpark.

For a little whippersnapper, Curious George books are easy to build a theme around. Check out his antics at a candy factory (give with fancy chocolates or candy-making supplies), or making pancakes (include a mix, fresh blueberries, a pancake turner, and bottle of real maple syrup), or at the zoo (tuck in a stuffed animal and some gummy creatures or animal crackers).

Your turn! Name someone on your list. Ask yourself, "What is a book they'd delight in reading?" Now . . . build your basket. GO!

know the Bible never mentions that there were three kings [or magi]? It is just assumed there were since there were three gifts.)

> **Christmas began in the heart of God. It is complete only when it reaches the heart of man.**
>
> ~ *Author Unknown*

When my kids were younger, the categories were: one toy to play with, one book to read, and one item to wear. This has evolved as our kids have gotten older. Trust me, the "one thing to play with" gets more expensive as they move into their teens!

Over the years, we heard about others doing this idea, often with a twist that ties in to the nativity story. So we morphed our tradition into a gold gift, a frankincense present, and a myrrh package. Here is the concept:

Gold. This, like gold, is a highly desired item; something precious, maybe even pricey (thus my annual shenanigans on Black Friday—trying to secure the best deal).

Frankincense. Because real frankincense was burned during prayer and rose heavenward, the gift in this category is something that will draw them closer to God. Perhaps a new Bible, a Christian book series, a CD, an MP3 player loaded with Christian music, or tickets to an event or worship concert.

Myrrh. Myrrh is a burial spice used to cover the whole body. So the myrrh gift does the same thing. It goes on the body. In past years this has been rain boots and a new coat for Kenna, a favorite Detroit Tigers jersey for Mitchell, and a hunting jumpsuit and camouflage boots for Spence.

By following this tradition, we have opted out of the "keeping up with the Joneses" contest that often takes place each year. Our kids don't beg for tons of items since they know there is a limit on how many we will buy.

Gold, frankincense, and myrrh. Give it a try!

BEING AHEAD OF THE REINDEER GAMES

Here are some plan-ahead ways to bring a little more calm and a little less chaos to your Christmastime.

• • • • • • • • • Renee Swope • • • • • • • •

Proverbs 31 Ministries

Plans for the perfect Christmas danced across the stage of my mind. My mom, my brother, and my husband JJ's parents were coming to see us. Plus my dad and his wife would be here Christmas day, and JJ's brother and family were coming too. Inviting our out-of-town families to our home for the holidays for the first time was a dream come true. The fact that they could all come at some point between Christmas and New Years was just short of a miracle. I'm so embarrassed to admit this, but by the time everyone got there I couldn't wait for them to leave. In the midst of all the preparations, I'd gotten tangled up in Christmas lights and unrealistic expectations.

It all started when my husband and sons petitioned for blinking colored lights on the tree. *We don't do colored lights on the tree. I am a "white lights" kind of girl*, I insisted. But then JJ suggested our decorating decisions should be a "family activity" that year. *Who was this man and why had he not brought this up in pre-marriage counseling*? I wondered. The control freak in me started to freak out. *Don't get in the way of my perfect Christmas with white lights that make me and my home feel peaceful.*

Further attempts to have the perfect house, perfect menu, and perfect table settings were stealing my holiday joy. This being my first time hosting a holiday dinner, I'd failed to notice that my Christmas placemats didn't coordinate with my everyday cloth napkins, and I didn't have festive napkin rings. Worst of all, I didn't know how to cook a turkey.

In the midst of all the holiday obligations I'd placed on myself, I experienced one of my worst Christmas days ever. I had a house full of people but an oh-

Each time you are out at the grocery or department store from now until Christmas, think "stocking stuffers!" It is so much easier to find little, inexpensive items when you have weeks, or even months, of marked-down merchandise to choose from, rather than running out to purchase them all on Christmas Eve.

Buy your Christmas cards as soon as they are put on the shelves in October. Once a week, take just twenty minutes or so to begin addressing the envelopes while you watch television or a movie with your family.

so-empty heart. As I walked through my living room, picking up wrapping paper, I wondered why my dreams of the "perfect Christmas" hadn't come true. Many of the elements seemed to be in place: kids running around with remote-control cars, adults on the couch snoring to the tune of "Jingle Bells," and grown men playing sidewalk hockey in the driveway. We'd lit Advent candles and set out the nativities. Still, something was missing.

Trying to escape the holiday noise, I went upstairs to my bedroom and sat down on the floor in my walk-in closet. Taking a deep breath, I opened my Bible to read the Christmas story in Luke 2. Slowly, I let each word remind me of that first Christmas night and God's promise that came true in Bethlehem. "She gave birth to her firstborn, a son. She wrapped him in cloths and placed him in a manger" (Luke 2:7). A cross-reference led me to Isaiah 7:14: "The virgin will conceive and give birth to a son, and will call him Immanuel [God with us]."

Closing my eyes, I pictured Mary wrapping baby Jesus, her hands carefully folding each corner of cloth. Like a beautiful bow on the perfect Christmas gift, she placed a kiss on his forehead. That's when I realized what had been missing. In the hustle and bustle of creating the perfect Christmas, I'd forgotten to unwrap the perfect gift, the most important gift of all: the gift of Immanuel, God with us.

Bowing my head, I opened my hands and my heart, and unwrapped God's presence in my closet that day. I invited Jesus to bring calm to my anxious heart. To bring His perspective to my expectations and to help me enjoy the gifts of my family that were waiting downstairs. Simply pausing to acknowledge and thank Jesus for being with me brought peace to my heart unlike anything white lights and matching table settings could ever bestow. It ended up being the perfect Christmas after all!

Or, if you are going to run off labels on your computer, make it your goal every night before bed to enter in one or two addresses. It will seem like a less daunting task this way.

Most cookies and fudges freeze well, so start your holiday baking several weeks before Christmas. Then your treats will be ready to remove from the freezer and be packaged up for neighbors, teachers, service personnel, or visiting relatives.

Start now to center your heart on the real meaning of Christmas. Read the account of Jesus's birth in the Bible. This is found in Matthew 1:18–2:23 and Luke 1:26–2:52. Then read it again. Read it at least once a week, until many of the verses become cemented in your heart. This can enable you to stay focused on the real meaning of Christmas.

And finally, for a way-cool idea to tie Christ's birth, death, and resurrection together, if you have a real Christmas tree, don't get rid of it. Save it! Trim off the branches, leaving only the trunk, and then store it in an out-of-the-way place until it makes a grand comeback at Easter. (You'll have to peek at that section to see the great idea!)

Karen Ehman is the director of speakers for Proverbs 31 Ministries and an author of six books including *A Life That Says Welcome* and *Let. It. Go.: How to Stop Running the Show and Start Walking in Faith*. She has been the guest on national media outlets such as *Focus on the Family*, *Moody Mid-day Connection*, and *The 700 Club*. She has been married to her college sweetheart, Todd, for over twenty-five years, and together they are raising their three sometimes quarrelsome but mostly charming children in the boondocks of central Michigan. Though hopelessly craft-challenged, with pitiful, partially finished scrapbooks, she has won several blue-ribbon rosettes at the county fair for her cookies, pies, preserves, and breads. Connect with her for real-life encouragement at www.karenehman.com or inquire about having her speak at your event by contacting Proverbs 31 Ministries at 877-P31-HOME.

Glynnis Whitwer is executive director of communications for Proverbs 31 Ministries. She is one of the writers of *Encouragement for Today*, the Proverbs 31 email devotions, with over 600,000 daily readers. She is the author of *I Used to Be So Organized*, *When Your Child Is Hurting*, and *Work@home: A Practical Guide for Women Who Want to Work from Home*. She is also coauthor of a Bible studies series entitled Kingdom Living. Glynnis and her husband, Tod, live in Glendale, Arizona. They have five children, ranging in age from mid-teens to early twenties. Glynnis has a degree in journalism and public relations from Arizona State University, and worked as a PR writer before joining the staff of Proverbs 31 Ministries fifteen years ago. She blogs regularly at www.GlynnisWhitwer.com.

Proverbs 31
MINISTRIES

If you were inspired by *Everyday Confetti* and yearn to deepen your personal relationship with Jesus Christ, we encourage you to connect with Proverbs 31 Ministries. Proverbs 31 Ministries exists to be a trusted friend who will take you by the hand and walk by your side, leading you one step closer to the heart of God through:

- *Encouragement for Today*, free online daily devotions
- Daily radio program
- Books and resources
- Dynamic speakers with life-changing messages
- Training for women called to speak, write, and lead

To learn more about Proverbs 31 Ministries,
visit our website, www.Proverbs31.org.

Proverbs 31 Ministries
630 Team Road
Matthews, NC 28105
www.Proverbs31.org

EASY, AFFORDABLE WAYS TO MAKE AND KEEP
YOUR FAVORITE MEMORIES

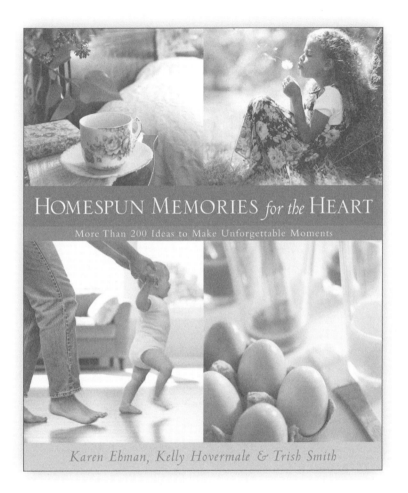

Homespun Memories for the Heart offers more than 200 inventive ideas and examples to help you make unforgettable moments, from growing sunflower playhouses to creating alphabet prayers and garden parties.

 Revell
a division of Baker Publishing Group
www.RevellBooks.com

Available Wherever Books Are Sold
Also Available in Ebook Format

GREAT HOSPITALITY ISN'T ABOUT GOURMET FOOD OR GORGEOUS DÉCOR
(WHAT A RELIEF!)

A Life That Says Welcome helps you make others feel refreshed, rather than impressed, in your presence. It's packed with inspiring tips and how-tos. You'll be encouraged not only to open your home but to open your life as an avenue for God's love everywhere you go.

KARENEHMAN.COM

Revell
a division of Baker Publishing Group
www.RevellBooks.com

Available Wherever Books Are Sold

"A woman with a confident heart chooses to believe that God wants to make an impact through her life, and she looks for ways to let him. Think about the things that make your heart come alive."

—*Renee*

Join Renee to enhance your personal study of *A Confident Heart* with the new *A Confident Heart DVD* (perfect for small groups!) and *A Confident Heart Devotional.*

RENEESWOPE.COM

Revell
a division of Baker Publishing Group
www.RevellBooks.com

Available Wherever Books Are Sold
Also Available in Ebook Format

Be the First to Hear about Other New Books from REVELL!

Sign up for announcements about new and upcoming titles at

RevellBooks.com/SignUp

Don't miss out on our great reads!

Revell

a division of Baker Publishing Group

www.RevellBooks.com